WOMEN
AT ARMS

Mrs. Maria Graeff with Colonel Ghadafi. (D.R.)

Maria Graeff-Wassink

WOMEN AT ARMS

Is Ghadafi a Feminist?

DARF PUBLISHERS
1993

English edition 1993
© Maria Graeff-Wassinck
First published in 1990 by Librairie Armand Colin, Paris
Translated from the French by Elio Bracuti

British Library Cataloguing-in-Publication Data
A catalogue record for this book
is available from the British Library

ISBN 1 85077 158 8

Cover design by Sue Sharples

Typeset by Hewer Text Composition Services, Edinburgh
Printed and bound in Great Britain
by BPCC Wheatons Ltd, Exeter

Contents

Part One
THE HISTORICAL AND
IDEOLOGICAL CONTEXT

Contents

Illustrations

Foreword

Libyan women and power

The word "Jamahirya" literally means the State of the masses. Are we to regard it as a neologism or an authentic innovation, or as barbarism from the Barbary Coast? At any rate, north of the Mediterranean an enormous amount of prejudice has grown up against the Ghadafian universe – some see it as pure and hard, others as perverse and diabolical, most see it as terrorist and threatening. On this side of the Mediterranean we find almost nothing but antagonism, incomprehension and hostility towards the Leader of the Libyan revolution.

But what about in Libya itself? Ask the women – daughters of camel-drivers, Berber farmers, or well-off middle class inhabitants of the towns founded by Ancient Greece and the Roman Empire, many of them thank "Brother Moammar, the liberator of women" . . .

"I don't have the temperament of a militant, but I willingly acknowledge that I have become what I am because of Ghadafi". This is how my first Libyan interviewee, a doctor in science from the University of Grenoble, now a lecturer at the El Fatah University in Tripoli, put it.

These words, in the form of a profession of faith, are very characteristic of the feeling of the women towards the Leader of the Revolution.

A second remark, this time made by a real militant, the

11

Secretary of the Revolutionary Committee of a Libyan society, corrects the first in a singular manner: "Women are not real revolutionaries, they work mainly for themselves".

After being based in Tripoli for almost two years, I began to see a clearer outline of the image of Libyan women and their role in the Jamahiryan revolution. Despite the almost total ban – at least at that time – on Libyans mixing with foreigners, particularly those from diplomatic circles, I was able to get to know more people, which was of great help in my understanding of the situation. This result was achieved by determination, perseverance, stubbornness, and even sometimes cunning. And if I had not had a minimal knowledge of Arabic, most of my contacts would have been, if not impossible, at least sterile.

Libyan women claim to be attached both to numerous new ideas (introduced by Ghadafian theories) and to ancestral traditions (still very much alive in this young country), and so appear in often contradictory lights. In this respect they are representative of Libyan society as a whole.

Libya is a country of contrasts, and Libyan women demonstrate contrasted femininity. They are at the same time revolutionaries and guardians of traditions. They wear the military uniform by day and the farashia by night[1]. For somebody who is just passing through here, the image of Libyan women is difficult to define, and even more so to decipher. First impressions often lead to mistaken interpretations.

The wearing of the "farashia" is like an ambiguous symbol of the uncertain situation of Libyan women today. Every woman, even the most modern and the most militant, receives this traditional costume when she marries (not to mention gold jewellery etc), which she will wear on all occasions in social life requiring a certain ceremony.

This was the case at one of the first very official occasions I attended, organised in the largest hotel in Tripoli by the "Ittihad Nissa'i Libya" – the Union of Libyan Women – and the Secretariat (Ministry) of Social

---

1 The farashia is the cloak of fine white wool which envelops the whole body and covers part of the face.

Affairs, to debate the rights of women in the Jamahirya. The organisers had wanted to give this "working meeting" somewhat of a party atmosphere – fanfare, procession of children wearing regional costumes, platform decorated with flowers, and a fancy buffet. Of course, most of my "suffragette" friends from the Ittihad were wearing their traditional costumes and the farashia. But when they came out, at about two in the morning, they took the wheel of their own cars to go back home, alone. Without doubt the next morning most of them put on their European-style dress as usual.

The most obvious trap for the "non-participating observer" which I then was is to assimilate the observed fact to this or that situation previously encountered, which is cut off from its original context. So at the beginning of my time in Tripoli I was tempted to compare these young Libyan women of today to the Moroccan students to whom, twenty years earlier, I had taught social psychology in Rabat and Fes. Such a comparison could only distort any analysis. There is no common measure between the political and social context of Morocco in the 1960s – where Hassan II was trying out a certain experiment in Westernisation – and what was represented in 1982 by "the State of the Libyan masses", where the charisma of the Leader of the Revolution for one thing, and the desire to please him for another, were in no way foreign to a local feminist current claiming to be revolutionary. So the "model" of women – developed, emancipated and liberated – was there and then radically different, notwithstanding the restrictive traditional Arab–Moslem environment common to both.

For Moroccan women, the inspiration came largely from the West (France) taken as reference and example. For Libyan women in the 1980s, the source was mainly political – the precepts and slogans of the *Green Book*. So how does the transfer take place from norms to practice, from teaching (indoctrination?) at school and university to daily life, from the revolutionary archetype to development of habits and customs? How do these women judge their own situation? Do they wish profoundly to follow the revolutionary path, the path traced by Colonel Ghadafi's *Green Book*? Do they want to go further (or not so far) in the direction of their liberation? What obstacles do they come up against? And what internal conflicts – family or conjugal – are concealed in this emerging, largely experimental, society? So many questions without answers, which aroused the (natural or professional?) curiosity of a woman researcher in social sciences, for whom the study of female identity has, throughout a winding course, remained a continual interest. On the fringe of the French system because of my training abroad (the Netherlands), buffeted about by the chance nature of a diplomatic husband's postings, therefore handicapped and privileged at the same time, I have always felt close to, if it was not my own state, the condition of women seeking identity and cultural synthesis (mixed marriages, opposition of careers between partners, situations producing interaction between observer and observed etc).

In Tripoli in 1982, I seized the opportunity presented by my position as permanent representative in Libya of the "United Towns Organisation," a world federation of cities, to establish working contacts with the mayors and their colleagues in the town councils concerned. Following these initial formal contacts, during the five years of investigation and study, the Libyan authorities gave me their trust and assistance on an intellectual as well as material level. Without this positive support which helped me to overcome barriers and obstacles, which encouraged me to persevere in the effort despite sometimes strong reticence on the part of certain groups or individuals, which finally led me to overcome the periods of doubt marking this course, the work of investigation and research could not have reached its conclusion.

How could I also not express my gratitude to the authorities and the students at the Women's Military Academy. Despite the inevitable misunderstandings and incomprehension at the beginning, I was able to develop, inside this unique environment, so jealously guarded from foreigners' eyes, sometimes as a part patched onto the "staff", and sometimes as a temporary "companion in arms", acceptable and quite well accepted.

I also owe much to my colleagues and certain authorities at the El Fatah University in Tripoli – particularly the Director of Research – who advised me on the organisation of the surveys and conduct of the investigation in a student environment.

I owe a very special acknowledgment to the loyal and generous Endira, who was my kind interpreter throughout the study. Although herself a foreigner, but brought up in Tripoli and totally integrated into the different Libyan circles, she taught me to understand and to love this people whom she chose to serve as a journalist and announcer for French language radio and television.

I want to mention finally the staff and management of the World Centre for Study and Research into the Green Book, who from the very start opened wide the doors of their institute, their library, their offices, their secretariat, and who, too, gave me their friendship.

Finally, last but not least, this book would not have seen the light of day without the personal interest and effective support of Colonel Ghadafi, who demonstrated his concern for the quality of a study devoted to Libyan women and their role in the Jamahirya, and who on many occasions showed great patience when its methodological and technical aspects were being discussed.

On the French side, I should not omit to express my thanks to those male and female colleagues whose advice, criticism, and corrections greatly helped this work to mature, to find a structure, and to reach – despite inevitable gaps and imperfections – the form through which an intellectual and personal experience can be communicated. In particular I would like to mention socio-analysis, the development of which I have known and followed for many years. Its concepts have given me a framework of interpretation which has helped me, in a complex situation, to master the inter-action between the observer and the observed and to understand power in actuality[2].

---

2 See in particular Chapter V, Part II: "A global strategy to change mentalities".

Introduction

Libya is still a country which has not been studied to any great extent and is not very well known. It is often perceived solely in a negative way. To reduce the Libyan regime, as is almost always done, to a totalitarian and dictatorial, even "terrorist", regime hardly serves to improve knowledge and understanding of the country. This requires a maintained effort of analysis and in-depth research, as it is a society in a state of evolution and total transformation.

Christiane Souriau, who was one of the leading specialists in contemporary Libyan society, already expressed this some years ago: "The reality of Libyan society is totally unknown. The world only knows stereotypes broadcast by the mass media – oil, petro-dollars, fundamentalist Islam, Ghadafi's personality, the desert, etc. The reality has many more nuances and variations – a very young population in a state of full evolution, hardy and heterogeneous, a political and social formula representing an original experiment in democracy."[1]

Of the five countries in North Africa, Libya is without doubt the one undergoing the greatest social change in the shortest period of time. An experiment which claims to be unique has been taking place for fifteen years on the scale of a

1 Christiane Souriau: "Femmes et politique en Libye", Revue francaise d'Etudes Politiques Mediterraneennes, 3rd quarter 1977, no. 27.

nation in gestation. "Jamahirya", a word coined by Colonel Ghadafi, "Leader of the Revolution", indicates a social project which is establishing itself based on a direct democracy.

This democracy seems first of all to be shaped by Bedouin life and original Islam. It also sets out to integrate other political concepts – those of the Ancient Greek city and Helvetian democracy, for example. Furthermore, and unlike other revolutions (particularly the revolutions of the 18th and 19th centuries in Europe), the Libyan revolution explicitly demands the participation of women in its programme and construction of the new society. Many of Ghadafi's speeches proclaim this: "Democracy will re-discover its rights when women decide their fate in the same way as men decide and organise their life", and also, "The Jamahirya is the society of all the people and not of men only".

Despite certain appearances and in particular with regard to women, Libyan society is thus no longer solely based on archaistic and patriarchal values. Although collective life there still develops around the family, which continues to be the centre of gravitation for social life, the majority of girls are no longer brought up only to become wives and mothers. Not only do they receive the same education as boys (primary and university education are mixed, secondary is on the way to becoming so) and can almost always take advantage of the same professional training as young men (including a military career), but they are also and very officially encouraged to take part in public, social and political life.

Although it is true that until now few women have worked outside the home, they are no longer reduced to remaining for their whole life no more than the daughter of X, the sister of Y, or the wife of Z. In principle, in the Jamahiryan system, every woman must be able, if she desires, to play her role and take her place as an independent person choosing her own path, a path which may lead, in the extreme, to a status of being single by choice. This is the case in particular of the "revolutionary nuns"[2] – which for anyone with any knowledge, however little, of the Arab and Mediterranean world, represents a new state of social relationships and constitutes a remarkable evolution.

2 See Part 2, Chapter IV.

Our reason for choosing the Women's Military Academy for study in the first part of an investigation aimed at discovering this hidden side of the Libyan nebula was that this institution seemed to us symbolic of the system.

The main interest in the Women's Military Academy lies precisely in this aspect as a symbol. As a military institution it is on the fringe of society, properly speaking there is a gap between it and contemporary Libyan society as such. However, insofar as this innovative experiment teaches us about the tactics applied by Colonel Ghadafi in his strategy for transforming society – its intrinsic value and its limits – it adds to our knowledge of the realities of the Jamahiryan system. This study also aims to make a critical contribution to the understanding and identification of the transformation process in Libyan society today. The emancipation of women de facto fits into the general context of reorganisation of a society with special characteristics, a society presented as popular and socialist by Ghadafi in his doctrinal work, the "Green Book".

Research conditions in Libya
Methods applied during the study

With the advantage of proximity due to exceptional circumstances – a three-year stay, devoted more to relationships outside university, putting us in a position to acquire opportunities for contact and human relationships within the least open compartments of the social edifice – we tried to record systematically the phenomena observed. This enabled a double obstacle, of a theoretical and practical nature, to be overcome:

– an obstacle often obstructing the access paths to an empirical observation approach,[3]

– a specific obstacle, as we were dealing with a sector which is considered sensitive in any country – the army as a professional institution and environment.[4]

But it is not a priori easy to carry out individual interviews in

---

3 Choice of sample, methods and content of individual interviews, interpretation procedures.

4 Despite a verbal but formal authorisation from Ghadafi himself, following presentation of a research plan regarding the training tool of the "women at arms", the local military authorities were for a long time reticent contrary to the nihil obstat from the Supreme Leader.

Libya in appropriate observation conditions i.e. in a "neutral" location, away from a hierarchical presence, with a dispensation from informing the authorities of the details of the questions selected, and as only recourse the presence of an interpreter[5] who was not Libyan but had been brought up in the country.

However, long and delicate negotiations enabled us to overcome reticence, to forge invaluable personal connections, to establish a certain trust, and in short to create the minimum conditions necessary for the different phases of the research to be carried out successfully.[6]

Methodological remarks

Any human phenomenon contains indivisibly a triple historical, social and personal dimension, and men themselves as autonomous individuals and social beings develop their activities both in time and in space. We have tried to combine such basic data from our own observation position.

Thus we first sought to study the behaviour of individuals linked to their integration in a particular community at a specific time. We completed this approach by an analysis of the factors and agents of the social change. Some incursions into the past seemed indispensable to us to fit the determining facts of the social development of Libya since its independence into their history.

These complementary and coordinated points of view enabled us to put the emphasis on the links connecting individual behaviours, group phenomena and inter-subjective processes. We also sought to separate the components of the "social model", of which any innovation process implies emergence, and thus to clarify the possible direction of the future development of social relationships between the two sexes.

Ideology, by the social change that it seeks to generate, is itself an operative instrument. The case of Libya, where the formation of a new social identity represents one of the main stakes of the revolution, does not contradict this rule.

To define this stake we had to vary the methods and

5 Taking into account the difference between the Libyan dialect of Arabic and the classical language used by the author.

6 Spread over four years, they required no less than six study trips after the end of the stay.

instruments of research. As far as possible we based our research on existing documents – historical or historising – from various sources. We attached particular importance to the corpus of speeches, conferences and other public statements of Colonel Ghadafi.

To carry out our research – ground research – away from theoretical approaches or school methods, we used mainly the interview methods, according to three variants, as follows:

– the free interview around a framework (for the students and staff of the Academy);

– the group interview to define the image of the Academy in the eyes of the outside world, in particular in the civil environment;

– the interview by questionnaire (with male officer students, to determine their attitudes towards women at arms).

In order to define our sample in relation to all the students at the Women's Military Academy, the individual interviews (15) were preceded by the circulation of a brief questionnaire to all the students (130).

To evaluate the development of mentalities in a military and non-military environment, we designed a test questionnaire adapted to the Libyan context, and submitted it to representative samples of the Academies and the University. This test, which presented a series of conflict situations (between a girl and her parents, a woman and her husband) gave the interviewees[7] the choice between several pre-coded responses.[8] From a detailed statistical and qualitative analysis of the responses, we tried to measure the impact of ideology on the development of mentalities and to assess the distance still to be covered on the path of the proposed social model.

It is true that the heavy dependency on the interview method, whose limits of validity are known, imposed precautions. So, to better control the factors induced by having many interviewers, we decided on the principle of having the identity of the interviewer constant. Furthermore, for the interviews around a framework, we tried to remove rigidity

---

7 180 interviewees.

8 Some referring to the old patriarchal standards, others to the alternative values prescribed by the Jamahiryan ideology.

by changing the order of the questions and introducing a conversational environment.[9]

Although the military management did not prove itself to be very open to respecting the rules and conditions of research, we did, however, meet a lot of understanding and effective support from the Libyan teachers and researchers in social sectors.

As for the reactions of the interviewees themselves, we noted their complete lack of familiarity with the practice of surveys and opinion polls. Although we did not exactly meet with refusals, the unusual nature of the situation for them could not but slow down a little the beginning of the discussion.

The interest, even curiosity, of the interviewees, military as well as civil, led in many cases to expanded discussions and debates. Whereas ground studies are rarely practised by Libyan researchers, several social science students demonstrated their strong interest in survey techniques by asking their teachers, for example, to teach them the method.

Working programme

In the first part we apply ourselves to situating the characters and the events in their historical context and their theoretical frame. It is thus important to put in perspective the development of the structures and organisation of Libyan society, from the time of King Idriss until the advent of the "Libyan Arab Republic" and its transformation into the "Jamahirya". In particular we relate the changes that have occurred in the advancement of women as a significant sector in social development, a pivot and key in the modernisation which is desired and imposed by Colonel Ghadafi. As we are dealing with the "woman at arms" we try to distinguish the myth from the reality, integrating both into the history of the changes that the Libyan army has undergone since the country became independent in 1951. Then

9 Being concerned about symmetry (equality), at the beginning of the interview we always promised to give the interviewee the opportunity to in turn question us, at the end of the interview.

The majority of the subjects took this opportunity and multiple questions were put to us (by men as well as women) regarding, for example, the life and status of women or relationships between young people and girls in France or Holland (my native country). Sometimes the questions posed were more personal – Would I myself have liked a military career? Would I allow my own daughter to enrol in a Military Academy?

we show the successive stages of the change in the status of Libyan women, of a patriarchal nature in traditional society, and which is declared to be egalitarian in the present. This first part thus allows us to paint the characteristics of the model of society, the "State of the masses", as Moammar el Ghadafi has been striving to establish it since 1977.

The second part of the book is devoted to the symbolic object of the advancement of Libyan women – the Women's Military Academy. A classic Jamahiryan institution, the Academy is intended to train the élite officers of "women at arms". But it has also, and in particular, an implicit function of creating a new model of woman, indeed a new image-guide for all women, Libyan, Arab or others. The woman officer belongs to the new élite, the privileged reference categories in the service of the revolutionary ideology. We note, moreover, that the training of women officers is only one of the instruments designed by Colonel Ghadafi in order to provoke a change in mentalities. Other new female élites – members of the Revolutionary Committees, Jamahiryan bodyguards, revolutionary nuns – run side by side with the officers from the Military Academy, to incarnate the new model and disseminate the ideology. In this way the contours take shape of an overall strategy which, in the area of social change, seems to be the distinctive mark of the Ghadafi practice.

Extending our field of observation, in the third part we analyse the impact of Ghadafi's feminist ideology on the young Libyan generation. For this purpose we have proceeded to carry out surveys to situate the development of mentalities on the level of the male military academies as well as university institutions. Our aim was to assess, from the standard sample of women officers, the development of the mentalities of their male counterparts, but also male and female students in civil society.

In conclusion, we aimed to propose elements of interpretation of the feminism of Moammar el Ghadafi, in order to clarify some key questions which seem essential to us:

– By what fundamental motivations can we explain the choice of the Libyan leader in favour of the feminist programme as a lever of the revolution?

– From what deep forces comes the option of the "woman at arms" as a model and image-guide for all advancement of women?

23

Cyrene

Leptis Magna

PART ONE

THE HISTORICAL AND IDEOLOGICAL CONTEXT

It would not be possible to situate the Libya of today, a country which is nevertheless still difficult to get to know and to penetrate, without clarifying by history the uncertain path from its past to its present, and without leaving the well-beaten tracks. For a long time ranked among the poorest regions of the world, the three provinces which make up Libya – Tripolitania, Cyrenaica and Fezzan – were, thanks to the fortune brought by oil, to pass almost without transition from the age of the bada'oui (nomads) and the muduni (city dwellers) of Ibn Khaldoun to all the excesses of decreed urbanisation and unrestricted consumerism.

To go back in the case of Libya is to travel through the space-time separating a traditional Mediterranean society dominated by a certain patriarchal-type opposition to change – nomadic, rural or urban – to the stage of a nation-state of blatant dynamism, upsetting all the compartments of the economic and social landscape.

Libya did not wait until 1969, the year of the coup d'état by Lieutenant Ghadafi, to announce the change. Through the centuries, following the example of its different neighbours from the "mare nostrum", this country, wedged between the Egyptian and Punic worlds, had begun the development and acceleration of its own history under various, but always exogenous, influences[1]. Some passed on certain common traits that it shares with other lands, continental or insular, of the area formed by the Mediterranean.

The fact that Libya belongs to the Arab-Moslem civilisation, such as it appears to us today – on linguistic,

1 See in particular J. Bessis "*La Libye contemporaine*", Ed. l'Harmattan, 1986.

religious and cultural bases – is indeed a determining factor but not the only one. Libya is an integral part of the continent of Africa. Without doubt Libya owes the dominant bedouin nature of its particular culture to the great Libyan-Berber tribes (to which a very old Saharan origin assigned, through their nomadic way of life, a connecting and communicating role between central Africa and the Mediterranean world). It is also from this specific environment, marked by a strong originality among the countries of North Africa, that the leader of the Libya of today appeared. Born far from the towns, in the vast spaces that edge the Great Sirte where the Sahara and the Mediterranean Sea run alongside each other without transition, the child Moammar grew up among the herds, as close as he could be to the universe of women which was to mark him strongly (his mother, his sisters, his aunts), before going late to join his tribe's school. Far from denying his Bedouin origins, the leader of the Libyan Revolution has always cultivated them, and has not ceased to nourish his vision thereof[2].

But through the thousands of years of intercourse, Libya also has something of the nature of the authentic patriarchal system, the principle of which is contained in the Old Testament, common source and sacred foundation of the three monotheistic religions. Thus links were woven, from Marseilles and Genoa to African Tripoli, from the Greek archipelago to Cyrenaica, which through the Barbary Coast epic transgressed the antagonistic interests of the Christian world to the North and the Islamic provinces of the Ottoman Empire to the South.

The terms of reference of this book do not allow us to develop further the ideas associated with what Fernand Braudel called "the long historic time". Let us just remember, with regard to the formative elements of contemporary Libya, that no-one could underestimate the importance and influence in the present state of the society of multiple cultural and socio-religious factors which had exercised conflicting effects through the ages. The fact is there are

---

2 On this subject it would be useful to consult *"La Geste hilalienne, version de Bou Thadi"* collected by Lucienne Saada (Ed. Gallimard 1985). This epic text, founder of a culture shared by the whole of the Maghreb world, is outstanding on the values of the Bedouin way of life.

abstract ingredients to the historic inheritance as well as remains of stones – they bear witness to the past for the present whether they are recognised or not[3].

In the chapters which follow we restricted our attention to giving a broad outline of the main events in the post-colonial period, when the coup d'état of 1 September 1969 divided the monarchy from the republic. From the country's independence (1951) to the revolutionary period, the vicissitudes of the regimes sometimes marked out, sometimes acted as framework and vital thread for the transformation of institutions, mentalities and customs. Thus we will successively review, keeping to the essential, the State's structures and their modification, as well as the changes in the military institution, in order to better situate the place of the family in society and the development of the status of women according to the Ghadafian concept of feminism.

---

3 Revolutionary Libya has not spontaneously integrated its roots and its sources into its singular history. Only by a slow effort, most often exerted from outside, is the pre-Arab/Islamic antiquity gradually recapturing a relative right of mention.

Chapter I

From the monarchy to the "State of the masses"

"It is more difficult for a country to keep its independence than to acquire it".

This statement is attributed to Mohammed Idriss I, put at the head of the kingdom of Libya created by the federative union of the three provinces of Cyrenaica, Fezzan and Tripolitania. When independence dawned on 21 December 1951, it was a militarily occupied territory, a country of the most fragile structures, with endemic poverty aggravated by war, which fell to the lot of the first sovereign of the illusory dynasty. Everything – State, nation, administrative centralisation, economic and social development, was to be invented to give this country an authentically Libyan government.

A long eventful past – three or four thousand years of Libyan pre-history and history – comprises all the diversity of ways of organising and governing the citadel. Should we incriminate the flow and counter-flow of migrations, conquests, invasions – and the secular re-shaping of the human elements, of the civilisation models resulting therefrom – in the fact that Libya today presents a unique laboratory of political experiment?

From time immemorial, since High Antiquity, the area of Libya has been conquered by foreigners. Libya has been bestowed with, coming from outside (the "two Mediterraneans" as Fernand Braudel puts it), the religious and cultural influences just as much as the politico-military violence and oppression. So there was the expansion of the Punic citadels and their Hellenic rivals; incursions of the barbarian hordes against the Libyan "pentapol"; the munificent domination of Rome, the domestication of the land by its incomparable legions, and after some centuries the threat from the great Vandal invasions; Byzantine expeditions; successive waves of the Arab conquest, and its decisive function as missionary for Islam; the incessant harassment of the shore by the chasing seacraft (Norman, Spanish etc) until the historic landing of the Turkish pirate Darghout Pacha at Zaoura (1551), a prelude to more than three centuries of more or less continuous domination of the Sublime Porte[1], which only ended with the annexation by Italy in 1911.

From this historic maelstrom contemporary Libya emerged. The Senoussian monarchy received it as exclusive right from jealous protectors, particularly preoccupied with investigations for oil. The Second World War had meanwhile marked the Libyan territory as if by a final incarnation, with its battlefields and huge military cemeteries which, as at Tobruk, bear witness for posterity.

The colonisation by Italy and the Allied military occupation had in no way prepared the Libyans – those of the towns and those of the tribes – for the modern forms of political expression (press, parties), and even less for the practice of any sort of democracy (elections). Slowly, after the end of the war, embryos of political and group organisations were going to emerge. Moreover, without any structured apparatus, the frustration nourished by hatreds accumulated under the military and police oppression of Fascist Italy found its first outlet in a Jewish-Arab confrontation (1945–1946), which very quickly ended in the demoli-

---

1 Under the Karamanli dynasty (1711–1835) Libya enjoyed extensive autonomy.

tion of the local Israeli community[2]. Later (1967–1972) fifty thousand or more Italian settlers left, as well as several thousand foreign experts, many of whom had thought they were installed for life in a Libya of two million inhabitants (density: 1.2 inhabitants per km^2).

On the level of political sovereignty, as in matters of defence and economy, the independence of Idriss I's Libya was quickly going to reveal itself to be formal, if not nominal. The accession to power of the tribal head had indeed reassured and satisfied the traditional clientele of Senoussi – religious authorities and great chieftains, of whom he was the natural protector, conservative and moderate circles in the urban centres of Cyrenaica, without forgetting the coterie of superior officers and English political advisers, to whom in the eyes of many his allegiance remained.

On the other hand, opposing his fragile power little by little, were most of the important people of Tripoli, as well as the circles motivated by strong pan-Arab and pan-Islamic sentiments, encouraged by Egypt and Syria. As for what was left of the tenure of an anti-Fascist Left, whose ideology crystallised around hostility to the Anglo-American "imperialism", the monarchy had hardly any difficulty in stopping its voice.

Idrissian Libya was especially subject to pressure from Egypt, where the victory of the "free officers" (July 1952) was soon followed by the advance of the "Unionists". It had to face their influence and at the same time the agitation of the Bathist groups, as well as the counter-blows of events in North Africa. The King very quickly suppressed and forbade the growing activity of the young political movements, which he pushed into semi-clandestinity.

From then on the kingdom was going to apply itself to promoting a mixed strategy: a prudent wait-and-see approach to the Unionist designs of Nasser, and support for North African independence and unity; alliance with Great Britain and the United States to protect itself militarily against the instability of the region and to have the benefit of substantial aid (financial, economic and technical) in

2 According to estimates, at Independence Libya had between 35,000 and 50,000 Jews. Today there are none left.

return for conceding military bases at Tobruk and Wheelus Field. The obsession with defence was thus at the origin of the first hitch at independence.

There is more. The alienation from the centuries of foreign occupation was replaced by that from the "free hold" of the oil companies on the country's tool for development. The arrival of oil production and industry was in ten years going to change the face of things in Idriss's Libya.

In 1959 (the first concession had been granted in 1955), oil flowed out at Zelten. Five years later, annual production stood at more than 40 million tonnes. Doomed a few years earlier to endemic under-development, Libya had become a new Texas; it did not take long to have nominally the highest revenue per inhabitant in Africa.

With this money, the country had a pressing need to modernise society. But the shock of the monetary economy revealed itself to be a destroyer of ancient and fragile equilibriums. Furthermore, the "oil revolution" by far exceeded the capacity for response – political, administrative and technical – of King Idriss's system. So, in this country of imperfect national unity, with very low population and almost non-existent élites, the impact of the oil manna did not take long to provoke perverse effects – an exodus from the countryside and galloping urbanisation with the development of shanty towns, bureaucratic corruption, invasion of foreign technicians, introduction of alcohol, development of prostitution etc. So much so that nothing was more pressing to prevent a destabilisation of the regime than to promote an extensive programme of social transformation.

If they had only imagined that the King and his ministers would quickly reveal themselves to be impotent to ensure mastery thereof. On the economic level, the vast majority of Libyans had the impression that all this was happening outside them; they remained on the edge of an enrichment (which was moreover not very apparent) from which the only ones to benefit were the entourage of the King and a few shrewd business people or traders. A real effort was indeed put into development; a fever for modernisation even took over towns, and to a far lesser extent the countryside. But the projects, badly prepared and carried out by technicians from America or Europe, only took slight account of the needs and aspirations of the population. Not to mention the fact that the investments, managed in a mediocre fashion or by foreigners to their advantage, were not always productive for the country.

As for political life, it was kept up in a semi-lethargy. The public domain was just starting to open up; a liberal but very formal constitution, a parliament held on a leash and suddenly dissolved (1964), xenophobic movements which were more or less contained, only represented a screen of modern democracy. It was late (Autumn 1967) when this paternalistic, conservative, wilfully despotic regime opened up posts within the government to young élites educated abroad. As for women, some legislative efforts had indeed been made on their behalf, such as access to public education or the right to vote, but they remained largely theoretical[3]. They in any case understood badly the confinement, the segregation and the exclusion from political life which traditionally affected them and isolated them from the action of men.[4]

While discontent and opposition to the monarchistic system were growing through student demonstrations, strikes, opposition from political groups, the emergence of new forces called on to snatch the Libyans from their apparent lethargy became unavoidable. We know that several plots were being worked on when a group of soldiers, young and unknown, carried out the coup d'état of 1 September 1969. Emulators of Nasser, they immediately gave themselves the name of "free unionist officers". The dynamics of the change that they were going to bring to the country in the sense of its modernity promoted a complete revolution and, what is more, a revolution which rapidly became established as a permanent revolution.

The first signs of the extent of the change did not take long to manifest themselves. Right in the first week of September 1969, a government of 9 members was formed

3 In 1968 the universities of Benghazi and Tripoli had 3,000 students, 330 of whom were women, i.e. 11%.

4 Even there where, for instance, under Ottoman domination, marriages with foreigners (cf. the Karamanli of Tripolitania) required them to "negotiate" with the intermediary power of the local dynasties.

under the management of the Council of the Command of the Revolution (CCR) presided over by Moammar El Ghadafi. The latter abolished the 1951 constitution, to replace it two months later with a "Constitutional Proclamation". Libya was from now on called the "Libyan Arab Republic". The political parties, already prohibited during the monarchy, continued to be so despite the pressure exercised by several political groups (Bathists, Marxists etc). This prohibition was justified by the urgency of the reconstruction of the country, which in no way gave the Libyans time to occupy themselves with partisan political intrigues.

As soon as power was taken over the new team also revealed itself to be concerned about both the needs and the opinion of all the layers of the population. Thus, consultation meetings were organised regularly in all the regions of the country.

It was in June 1971 that the CCR, which until then had governed the country alone, decided to create a real political organisation, largely copied on the Nasserian Egyptian model – "the Socialist Arab Union" (SAU), whose slogan was "Liberty, Socialism, Unity". The SAU claimed to be a popular organisation. It was supposed to pave the way for the take-over of power by the people themselves by providing them with a first participation in power and a first political experience. Without doubt it also aimed at giving Libyan society a political structure, at the time when the Arab Federation had just been formed (August 1972) with Egypt. Under the grip of the SAU, the system of political parties was rejected with even more violence – they even went so far as regarding the formation of a political party as a "criminal act". Slogans were launched: "The parties' system aborts democracy", "Parties weaken the nation and divide the peoples" etc.

It was at the beginning of 1973 that Ghadafi and his team, with the famous speech of Zouara, initiated the "cultural revolution". From this date, Ghadafi's ideas were going to be formulated, and his ideological concepts applied, in a more coherent form, designed for action – the "Green Book".

In its historical perspective, the Libyan revolutionary programme expressed firstly a desire for "reintegration of itself", which was something the previous regime had shown itself precisely to be incapable of taking on. The "Libyan Arab Republic" established the day after the monarchy was overthrown, did not so much bring a new law as it interpreted an existing situation, and attempted to adapt the traditional tribal institutions to the imperatives of modernisation and change. Through the new motto of "Liberty, Socialism, Unity" (precisely that of the Nasserians), it pursued its demand for identity by the re-approval of the national, Arab and Libyan inheritance both on the physical level (liquidation of foreign bases, nationalisation or "Libyanisation" of aircraft and colonial property, re-purchase of oil concessions) and the cultural-religious level (Arabisation, restoration of the "shari'a" as basis for the legislation, return to the "original Moslem city state" and to certain aspects of Bedouin society).

Right from the start, the Libyan revolution, like most revolutions, demanded a new society based on the equality and universality of men. And, like others, its ideology, by the very fact of its Utopian dimension, led to a constant pressure and control, in order to avoid the immediate reconstitution of the old inequalities. In Libya, as elsewhere, this aim of continuous revolution was accompanied by a cavalcade of denunciations, by a police climate, and finally by injustices. But this ideology denies being either nationalistic or particularistic, in the sense that those of Hitler's Germany or Ataturk's Turkey declared themselves to be.

The specific identity of the Libyan revolution lay rather in a social project which aimed at being universal, which rejected out of principle the synthesis between Eastern and Western civilisations, which were equally criticised. This project tried to offer a version of Islam at the same time fundamentalist and progressist, marked by the constant search for conciliation between a certain modernism and the fidelity to those traditions that did not hold up progress.

From then on the socialism which the new Libya was claiming must be understood as "social justice". Ghadafi gave the following definition of it, right at the beginning of the revolution: "Socialism is collective and continuous work, work done with devotion which leads us to a society of self-sufficiency and fair distribution, without exploitation, without theft and without inequality, without violating religious prohibitions, usury or pots of wine . . . " (16.9.1969). "Socialism is equality of opportunities, social justice and peaceful equalisation of the differences between the classes" (19.1.1971). But we should not make a mistake – in the end it comes down to an acceptance of socialism with a religious basis: "Islam is the religion of justice and real socialism . . . It introduced all the laws and doctrines valid for the good of Man before they were known by the rest of the world . . . " (idem: 19.1.1971).

It is indeed a theoretical model, an idealistic plan for society, but which started to be applied as early as 1973. The new speech pronounced at Zouara in fact marked the beginning of the real Ghadafian revolution[5]. This one was to be neither capitalist nor communist, it aimed to establish a "mass" society, in which the people would exercise sovereignty, in which power, wealth and arms would be put in the hands of the people. A deeply egalitarian society where each male and female citizen would also have their place as a member of a family and a tribe.

It was from this date that the "Popular Committees" were formed, which from then on existed at the level of the quarters, the rural centres, the municipalities, as well as in the public administrations, the companies, the universities and the professional groups. They represent "the will of the people who have taken power". Between 1973 and 1976 this system developed not entirely smoothly and without reserve, to finish, in 1976, with the transformation of the former "National Congress" into the "General Congress of the Libyan People". The Popular Committees then became the executive organ (General Popular Committees) and legislative organ (Basic Congresses). The representative system was categorically rejected, there were to be no elections, there would only be one form of option – the appointment of those who were to represent the people on the executive level.

It is true that the new State did not neglect to seek in nationalism the ideological caution which made the change acceptable. But at the same time it based itself on a set of

5 "The popular revolution begins today" (16.4.1973).

wider values, in particular by integrating the social demands of women and the feminist problem to the modification of the public domain.

Although the Popular Committees, set up as early as 1973, were able to progressively exercise their functions, the new organisation of society only appeared completely and definitively from 1977, the year when the first part of the "Green Book"[6] was published. It was on 2 March 1977, before the General Congress of the People, that the "Socialist Popular Libyan Arab Jamahirya" was proclaimed and the principle of "direct democracy", which had already become reality to quite an extent, found itself in some way legalised. By the neologism "Jamahirya" – literally "the State of the masses" – the colonel, who had become "Guide of the Revolution" expressed this basic idea that Libyan society would for each citizen be a society of participation.

Edited between 1977 and 1979[7], and adopted as a basic document by the General Congress of the People in 1979, the "Green Book" has since then formed a doctrinal and legislative framework for the Libyans which modulates their usual statutes and assigns their rights and their duties. It has thus formed the moral, social, economic and political framework of the new society. The "Green Book" refers neither to Islam nor to the Qu'ran – this new social project has the ambition to address, beyond the Libyan and Arab people, all humanity. It does not, however, infringe the dictates of the Qu'ran which remain the basis of the Libyan imago mundi; but it separates the divine principles from the human precepts, it being possible and necessary to subject the latter to the effort of interpretation (social justice, moderation of private property, self-sufficiency, peaceful removal of class differences).

The slogans of the "Green Book" summarise the programme well: "Democracy is the power of the people and not the expression of the people", "The consumers must become

6 The "Green Book" Part One: "The solution to the problem of democracy – the power of the people" – Moammar El Ghadafi.

7 The "Green Book" Part Two: "The solution to the economic problem – socialism" (1978) and Part Three – "The social foundations of the third universal theory" (1979).

Women's Congress, Tripoli, 1990

Women's Congress,
City of Tripoli section, 1990

the producers, but they will be associates not paid employees", "The house belongs to he who lives in it", "The land belongs to he who cultivates it" etc.

When, in 1979, Colonel Ghadafi drew up the balance sheet of the past ten years, he showed that he was completely clear as to the limits of his success – it is indeed a forward thinker who carried out the revolution and who continues to breathe life into it. "Our Jamahirya is not yet a popular Jamahirya" he stated. He also denounced the trend of his fellow citizens to become bourgeois, as well as their tendency to let themselves be deluded by the mirage of money which the manna of oil presently provides in abundance. He thus seems to be constantly inclined to shake their apathy, to fight against the facility and the spirit of profit, to announce like a challenge to the present the future spectre of the post-oil period: "Libyan society must transform itself from a consumption society to a production society in order to fully achieve socialism . . . Material comfort favours or reinforces the bourgeois mentality".

For more than fifteen years Ghadafi has been applying himself to warning about the private accumulation of capital, and to putting forward the "third universal path", the one which, between capitalism and Marxism, will revolutionise working relations, abolish the employer-employee conflict, organise the distribution of the social product by participation in the fruits of production and the reduction of savings.

This is a construction which is strictly speaking more co-operative, solidarist and populist than socialist stricto sensu. Whereas an overwhelming majority of the Libyan population would be satisfied to consume the excess, thanks to the increase in revenue from oil, the Jamahirya has regulated and continues to regulate, despite a semblance of liberalism, the satisfaction of needs by contracting the circulations, compressing the household budgets and, finally, drawing up the surplus wealth into large Pharoesque works such as the very expensive "Man-Made River".

Following the second oil shock, this regime which aimed firstly at organising deep transformations in the economic and social fields, by favouring the diffusion to the heart of the masses of the power of monetary purchase, quite quickly had to apply heavy braking pressure on the amounts spent on

41

public and private installations. It remains significant that despite the very heavy dependency of his country's economy on oil and its perverse effects, the Libyan "helmsman" has not ceased to preach effort for everybody and to organise the mobilisation of the working forces, including female, by transgressing the patriarchal system.

Having thus quickly analysed the development of the Libyan structures and concepts since it gained independence, we must examine in a more detailed manner the role assigned in the construction of the new society to an institution called on to be one of its central pillars – the "Army of the People".

Chapter II

From the classic army to the army of the people

To perceive the originality of the Libyan political options of today and to disentangle the workings of a collective desire for change that originally led a few young nationalist officers to revolt, it is necessary to take a brief look at the history of this country's army since its independence. For the changes which took place in the very concept of the military institution (forsaking the notion of "professional armed force" and promoting the "people in arms") are an integral part of the revolutionary plan.

In 1951, at the time of the foundation of the Libyan kingdom, the British and American troops installed in the country since 1943 guaranteed its external security. Furthermore, two para-military groups, the CYDEF and TRIDEF,[1] served under British command to keep internal security[2].

This situation was to last five years. It was only in 1956,

---

1 "Cyrenaic and Tripolitain Defence Forces".
2 Added to which there were three French companies and one police unit whose task was to keep order in the province of Fezzan until 1955.

for political reasons and not unconnected with the events at Suez and the war in Algeria, that an autonomous Libyan army was formed. The mandate it received was to ensure, together with the British and American troops still present[3], the external defence of the country.

This army, of approximately 5,000 soldiers, was put under the command of an officer of Iraqi-British origin. His officers were made up of volunteers who could only have come from an English or American military academy. It was in 1957 that the first Libyan military academy was opened in Benghazi (by royal decree of 22 June 1957). In 1962, still under the aegis of Great Britain, the Libyan royal navy was formed in its turn. It was declared then that for another ten years foreign officers – English or American in particular – could be part of the Libyan national army.

But the bloody events which occurred at Tripoli and Benghazi directly following the violent criticisms formulated by Nasser's Egypt[4] against the presence of Libyan foreign bases were to lead the English to reduce the number of their troops stationed in Tripolitania. (In 1965, they were still double the number of Libyan troops). At the same time, Great Britain undertook to reinforce the Libyan national army.

In August 1969, at the time when the revolution of the "Free Officers" occurred, the Libyan army was made up of approximately 10,000 men trained by officers all instructed by the British and in Great Britain. The Libyan army of this period was thus an institution designed and moulded from outside, somehow tacked onto the political, economic and social structures of the country. As was natural, its largely exogenous character could not but pose problems. The same applied to the duality with the existence of internal security forces, CYDEF and TRIDEF, still totally made up of members of the Senoussi tribes and operating as the King's praetorian guard. The latter, stronger in numbers (13,000 men in 1965) had received the mandate from the King to "control the army", an effective control which was exercised

---

3 At the time the Wheelus base was the largest American base outside the United States.

4 In relation to Nasser's speech of 22 February 1964, which denounced the use of Libyan foreign bases as supporting Israeli policy in the Middle East.

for example through nominations into the army of superior officers coming from the internal security forces.

In fact, because of its importance, this political game slowed down and, in the extreme, blocked the promotion of young officers trained in the modern academies. It is not difficult to imagine that in these circumstances young officers of medium rank, among them Captain Ghadafi and the other free officers, were made sensitive in the extreme by the burden of a double supervision – that on the one hand of the Senoussis, the King's proteges, more archaistic in spirit, and on the other hand the English officers, suspected of working more in the interest of their own country and the defence of the West[5] than in accordance with Libyan criteria.

This military dualism corresponded grosso modo to the existence of two geo-strategic zones – the shore, historically dominated by foreigners (successively the Ottoman, Italian and Anglo-American troops)[6], and the interior, a sort of vital space more or less held by the Libyan tribes and for which, under the Italian domination, irredentists like Omar Mokhtar were the symbol of resistance.

This situation of balance and rivalry, which continued to exist until September 1969, suddenly came to an end with the take-over of power by the free officers, which transformed the army into a political instrument. The Revolution was to integrate the King's militia to the Army, which from then on was to control them strictly. The evacuation of the Wheelus base in June 1970 put the lid on a twenty-year period marked continuously by the preponderant role of the foreign powers within the Libyan armed forces, themselves kept in a state of division and competition by a monarchic power which was largely feudal.

Originally, the Libyan army had been made up solely of volunteers. It was only in May 1967 that a law brought in compulsory military service for all men over 18. But until the fall of the monarchy this law was not applied, as the English had always given preference to a professional army of low numbers, technically well trained and "motivated".

5 Thus, in matters of air defence, it was stipulated that arms could only be used by British officers.

6 A North African proverb, quoted by Christiane Souriau, says, "The danger comes from the sea".

The law in question was kept after 1969. However, the army continued to recruit volunteers. When Libya became part of the Federation of Arab Republics in 1971, the Egyptian army was supposed to ensure the defence of its different members. At the time of the war against Israel (October 1973) – undertaken by Egypt without consultation with Libya, which was one of the causes of the conflict between Ghadafi and Sadat – Libya, detaching itself from the powerful eastern neighbour, was obliged to reinforce its own army. In May 1974 a compulsory military training period limited to six weeks was decided on; during the summer of the same year a first group of students was called on to carry out a period of training in the army[7].

The foreign policy factors were not the only ones to act in favour of bringing in compulsory military training; the internal political context played as big if not bigger part in the decision by the Libyan regime. Already, at the end of September 1969, in his Sabratha speech, Ghadafi spoke of the necessity to militarise the population and to democratise the military forces so that people and army became one and the same reality. These ideas were to progress little by little.

1974 was the year when the subject of "direct democracy" was introduced into political life, and it was followed by a whole series of structural reorganisation. In November 1974, the "Active Popular Forces" met in an assembly and defined in the form of resolutions the steps envisaged in the field of national defence. In particular, the application of the law regarding compulsory military service was encouraged, "in order to avoid the dangers which threatened the Arab nation from those who aspired to its resources and aimed to strike the revolutionary forces in the Arab world".

From 1975, the short military training became compulsory for all the civil servants, who were called on to undergo it on a rota basis. Under pressure from the religious authorities, the idea of applying it to women was given up at the time, and this was the start of a long confrontation between the Council of the Revolution and the religious authorities.

The importance attached to the participation of all the

7 Cf. H. Mattes "Von Der Pratorianergarde Konig Idriss I zum Konzept des bewaffneten Volkes, Orent. 26 Jahrgang no. 4, December 1985.

citizens in the compulsory military training is closely linked to a concept of direct democracy. Ghadafi explained himself at a seminar on general military training in Tripoli in October 1975: "When we talk about the new experience (of direct democracy), we also talk about general military training. When the people are free, we do not need to force them to defend themselves. A free people means a people willing to bear arms and to be trained to defend themselves. Just like in a family or a tribe, nobody obliges you to self-defence; but if somebody attacks you, all the members of the family are obliged to defend you. If a family only defended itself when forced to, you could say that this family is ignorant and has not understood the meaning of liberty. It is exactly the same here – when the people have to be forced to defend themselves, they do not deserve to live. We want to show the world that free peoples are capable of ensuring their defence themselves, without needing to apply a law on the military obligation". On this occasion Ghadafi was to introduce a distinction between the military training (short duration) and the compulsory service (18 months or more).

During the period 1975–1977, several significant events took place in the Libyan military organisation. An "Academy for Air Defence", constructed and equipped in a very modern way, and benefiting from the assistance of highly qualified foreign staff, was opened in Missourata in April 1975. Furthermore, the military training of the civil servants required a correspondence between civil and military "grades". In 1975 a law was brought in to settle this matter – any promotion in the army would automatically lead to a promotion in the civil service. Finally, at the beginning of 1977, a central official body was created which received the monopoly for the import of "security equipment". In parallel, a decree formally prohibited the introduction or the manufacture of arms in a private capacity in Libya.

Various declarations made by the Colonel in 1975, 1976 and 1977[8], clearly show the development that was coming to light in the concept of armed forces – according to his

8 Such as: "Defence in the Jamahirya is not put under the responsibility of one group of Libyans – as is the case with the classic army, which ensures defence on behalf of society – but under the responsibility of the people as a whole". "Al Sijil al Qaumi", Tripoli, 1977, p. 590.

ideological vision, the classic distinction between professional army and "people in arms" was to progressively disappear.

The official proclamation of the Jamahirya on 1 September 1977 allowed the notion of "people in arms" to be defined more precisely: "Arms in the Jamahirya are no longer the monopoly of a classic army as they are in other countries. Arms are now in the hands of all the citizens, men and women. Bearing a weapon is a right and a duty of each Libyan man and woman . . . The innovation behind all these events is that the power has been transferred to the hands of the people. For as long as this lasts, it will follow as an inevitable consequence that the arms will also be in the hands of the people . . . "[9]

It thus appears that the aim of the concept of "people in arms" was not only the defence of the country against external aggression. It also contained an internal dimension, that is the protection of the revolution by the armed popular masses. As early as 1973, Ghadafi had evoked this objective in the following terms: " . . . I will distribute arms to the popular masses who believe in the revolution. As for those who are against the revolution of the people, we will not give them arms, rather we will put the weapon against their chest. The whole people will thus be transformed into a popular militia . . . "

In a speech on 7 April 1977, given at the university of Benghazi, the subject of the defence of the revolution by the "people in arms" was again taken up and developed: "If a political struggle was declared, all the forces of the revolution would be called on to fight so that the cause of the people triumphed, without a distinction being made between soldiers, politicians, students or workers. When it is a question of a political problem, all the popular forces without distinction are called on to fight against the forces which are enemies of the people. Thus the power, the wealth and the arms are in the hands of the people".

One of the main difficulties encountered in achieving the concept of the "people in arms" lay in the lack of motivation of the popular masses themselves. In particular they demon-

9 Speech edited in "Al Sijil al Qaumi", Tripoli, 1978, p. 93.

strated little enthusiasm for voluntarily taking part in the periods of military training. Having noted this on several occasions, Ghadafi criticised this behaviour: "On the one hand you want modern tools, for example for air defence; on the other hand the engineers and technicians, but also the ordinary citizens, do not want to use these arms and prefer to call on Egyptian and other specialists. We have an insufficient number of soldiers. Why? Because we have not decided on forced recruitment . . . "

The resistance shown by the basic Congresses, who were reluctant to pursue the application of compulsory military service, was overcome during the Summer of 1977 owing to the increase in hostilities with Egypt. This military confrontation helped the Colonel to convince the basic Congresses of the necessity for a compulsory general service. The resolution then adopted stated that conscription did not cancel either general military training or the recruitment of popular militia; that the military academies would be assimilated to university faculties, and that consideration would be given to individual family circumstances. Furthermore, it was decided that the equipment for the armed forces – for the soldiers as well as the officers – would be improved.

In May 1978 a new law was announced on compulsory military training, replacing the one of 1967 which had never been really applied. The re-introduction of compulsory service was justified in several ways, but in his proclamations Ghadafi put the emphasis particularly on the "provisional" nature of this measure: "As soon as the State of the people in arms is achieved, the law establishing compulsory military service will be abolished".

From then on the militarisation of Libyan society was going to make rapid progress, affecting all the milieux or groups of population:

a) In the second cycle of school studies (15 to 18 years), the pupils – girls and boys – were to receive training twice a week relating in particular to fist fighting;

b) The pupils of the military secondary schools learned, under the aegis of professional officers, how to use heavy weapons. Each school moreover had a speciality; it was connected to a particular weapon (land defence, air defence etc). Its pupils were prepared to serve as assistants to the specialists in these weapons.

c) All the men depending on their age were henceforth compelled to have repetitive periods of training:

– between 18 and 35, they were to take part in general training each year, for quite a long period (some weeks);

– from 45 to 55, they were trained for the specific tasks of popular resistance;

– some of those over 55 were to take part in "mujahidine columns", operating, for example, as coastguards (some of whom remained permanently armed).

d) As for women, married or single, volunteers for military training, they were called to exercises several times a week in a school in their area[10].

As a result, when this programme was put into practice, it was going to make Libya into one of the best customers of the arms suppliers in the world[11]. Since the law on conscription was applied, the orders for new material rose sharply, all the more so because arms maintenance – particularly by the non-professional elements – was notoriously poor.

But what fate was meanwhile reserved for the regular army? Wasn't its official function from then on divided among the Jamahiryan institutions?

In his speeches, Colonel Ghadafi could not avoid the problem. This is how he was led to declare in April 1977, before the Benghazi students: "The army today is no longer a traditional army. Its new task is to train the popular masses and to help to create the 'armed people'. Arms can become a dictatorial instrument, and subject the people to the dictatorship if they are monopolised by only one part of the population . . . It is necessary to put the citizens in possession of all the arms to achieve the dream of the formation of a sovereign people, a free people, a people that really controls itself".

Later he was to be more precise: "It is necessary for us to have a secretariat (= ministry) for Defence, like a Secretariat for Industry, for Social Affairs and for External Relations. The Secretariat for Defence has to direct the general military

---

10 The fact is Ghadafi could not obtain the vote by the People's General Congress for compulsory training for all women.

11 Cf. USSR, France, Italy, Czechoslovakia, Brazil.

training, deal with its organisation, and manage the inheritance; it must be responsible for the distribution and storage of arms, for the options on the tactics of war, for the division of the population into defence sectors. It must train the military officers needed for that".

It thus appears that the role of the army would henceforth be of an essentially technical nature; its main function would be tasks of organisation, training and supervision.

However, from 1 September 1969 to 1975, the year of establishment of direct democracy, the army had been the unique shield of the revolution. For all that, with the creation of the basic Congresses in 1975, the question had arisen whether there was a place or not for the militaries to be integrated into this system. Although the latter had obtained the right to participate effectively in the basic Congresses, and consequently the General Congress, the decision to establish "the army of the people" (a decision taken by the General Congress) had threatened to strip the army of one essential attribute of its power: the monopoly of arms. The formation of thousands of Revolutionary Committees and "Jamahiryan Guards" in March 1979 was, moreover, going to openly deprive the army of its particular function of protector of the revolution. The army thus found itself thereby even facing real counter-powers.

So the transition from the classic army to the popular army was revealing itself to be in no way an easy thing. Much more, it was not exempt from risks, as events subsequently showed. This has been shown since 1973 by a long series of acts of rebellion[12], demonstrating both the refusal of part of the army to accept a reduced status, and the effective reality of the power of the militarised popular organisations, as machines of control and counter-power.

It is true that they did try hard to compensate the professional soldiers for loss of status by material advantages, in the extreme turning them into the most pampered citizens of the Jamahirya. Special shops richly supplied with imported goods at subsidised prices were put at the

12 The aborted putsch in 1975, the flight to Egypt of Commander Mheichi, the Tobruk rebellion in August 1980 are the most well known.

disposal of the military and their families, also accommodation programmes, officers' clubs etc. But this situation would in turn not take long to create new tensions, this time with the revolutionary militia who started to denounce, rightly or wrongly, the "decadence" of the professional army as well as the excesses of all kinds which they claimed it generated. The editorial of the Zahf el Akhdar of 21 March 1983 did not beat about the bush – it demanded nothing less than "the destruction of an institution which is a haven for Fascists and degenerates devoting themselves to smuggling hashish, alcohol and pornographic films, without forgetting to traffic in influence, and all this instead of defending the homeland".

Was this a latent war between the militia and the regular army, or an indirect warning and threat from the "Management"? In any case it was important and urgent to prepare for the replacement of the old officers by a new generation, brought up in the spirit of the Jamahirya. This was henceforth going to be done actively through the activity of the military academies and schools, and also partly by sending trainee officers to certain countries in Eastern Europe.

It was on 31 August 1988, at a meeting of students from the military academies, that the abrogation of the traditional army (as well as that of the police) was officially proclaimed. The next day, 1 September, the 19th anniversary of the revolution, Colonel Ghadafi was to explain what seemed like the ultimate stage thus: "We seriously want to establish peace, one which is based on the exclusion of any possibility of war, and not on fear of the nuclear threat . . . To demonstrate our desire for peace, we are today dissolving the regular army to bring in the armed people, who can neither be conquered nor invaded". Expanding on his words, he added: "Humanity carries on living in fear instead of living in peace. Only the destruction of the armies will make it possible to achieve peace, with the establishment of armed people, only wanting to defend themselves, not to attack others".

The step had thus been taken. From then on it was the responsibility of the "people in arms" – that is the "Popular Committees" – to take care of all the missions aiming at local popular security. Until then controlled by professional officers, the defence areas would be controlled by the said committees. As for the traditional army and police, they were to be reorganised into a professional body which would take the name of "Jamahiryan Guard", whose function would be to assist the "people in arms" technically. A national short-term service, would take care of the duties.

On 1 September 1988, after a fifteen-year co-existence, the slow transformation from the classic army into the army of the people was officially completed. The duality of the institutions, which had already ceased to be regarded as such by the young military generation, therefore theoretically came to an end.

A certain development in mental attitudes accompanied this transformation, as is shown by the interviews carried out three years before with some trainee officers, men and women. From their answers it already became apparent that they regarded the disappearance of the army as a necessary and normal thing, which would in no way diminish their role, conceived more and more as a role of techicians, trainers, indeed educators:

— "The army must disappear, there will only be the people in arms. We want to eliminate the idea of (professional) army."

— "The aim for us is not to have a grade, but to train the people in arms, so as to contribute to bringing the population closer and closer together."

— "Our aim is not to acquire a power over the others, as was the case in the past for foreign and Fascist armies. Here, everybody is part of the army; and we, the professionals, are its instructors."

— "When I wear the uniform in the street, I feel that I am part of the people in arms. The only difference is my level in technology".

— "Being the army is, above all, to protect the achievements of the revolution. We thing that it is not necessary for us to undertake any sort of war. What is necessary is to look after our defence".

Brought up with this idea, the young military generation seems inclined not to dramatise the definitive disappearance, today theoretically consummated, of an autonomous professional army. But this does not apply to the old ones. Their opinions, their spirits, although not coming within the field of this study, no less make up a political and social reality, which the present command has to and will have to necessarily take into account.

Chapter III

From the wife hidden away to the "woman at arms"

Between 1951 and now we can identify, according to the nature of the events, four periods of roughly ten years each, during which quite significant and profound changes were made to the status of Libyan women.

The first, from 1951 to 1960, is characterised by the search for identity and the option of belonging to the Arab-Moslem world. It helped women, at the price of their segregation being emphasised, to become aware of their diminished status, but which from then on was more obvious and explicit.

During the second half of the monarchical period, opinion took shape in favour of a timid modernism; the first legislation beneficial to women appeared, giving them access to education, and offering them modest participation in social and public life, within the strict limits of Islamic tradition.

A third period is represented by the first nine years of the Ghadafi revolution. Not only was protective and "positively discriminatory" legislation offered to Libyan women, particularly favourable to mothers, but also and especially they were directly called on to take a full part in the political construction of society and the development of the country. For all that, their real status was hardly to change fundamentally during these years.

It was during the fourth period, which began in 1978 after the advent of the Jamahirya, that a desire took shape to radically change mentalities, not only in women but also among men, by the emergence of new models, particularly the one of the "woman at arms". It was during this period that a start was made on overthrowing the patriarchal system by an effort which was not only formal but effective to transform relationships between men and women within the family and society.

We need to pause for a moment at the patriarchal system, a dominant ideology within the society even today.

The Libyan family[1], as the basic element of the tribal and traditional society, has for centuries been characterised by the patriarchate. According to the Islamic precepts of behaviour and organisation, its order was based on the different nature of the sexes, combined with the absolute authority of a *paterfamilias* or "Patriarch", incarnating both the primate of the Qu'ranic law and the defence against the outside world. The social function of women was identified with reproduction. Guaranteeing the identity of the extended family community, her morality became a cornerstone of this family order; her physical integrity became an essential value in biological continuity. This leads almost logically to the necessity for keeping the sexes apart from an early age, and the division into spheres – private and public – of the social space belonging to the family and to society.

To this functional separation of the sexes (infical) is added and superimposed the inevitable domination of men over women. The total dependence of women on men, an

---

1 By "family" we mean firstly the form and reality of the "extended" family, as opposed to the "nuclear" family (limited to the father, mother and children, which we see gradually being established in Libya).

almost permanent availability of women in their role as wife and mother, characterised the relationship of the sexes.

From puberty, a Libyan girl was no longer allowed to leave the family "haouch" (circle), and, particularly in urban environments[2], her separation was very strictly observed. She only left her home very occasionally, wrapped in the traditional costume (the "farashia"), under the protection (supervision) of a male representative of the family. Her upbringing was completely centred on her future roles as a wife and mother, her socialisation being from the start in subjection to men, and in relation to them (whereas the man's upbringing, however, was defined in the concept of his natural superiority).

The woman was thus refused status as an adult, being judged incapable of protecting and keeping herself.

Within the domestic space which she was accorded by the specific nature of her role, she was only left a restricted liberty, marked (like that of the men, moreover) by the patriarchal, therefore strongly hierarchical, model, imposing on her particularly respect and obedience of her elders[3]. This situation prepared the girl for what would be her double dependence throughout almost all her life as a woman: on men, and on the elders of her own sex.

This hierarchisation, which formed vertical relationships and one-way communications (from above to below) promoted interactions of an authoritarian type: orders and threats rather than negotiation, discussion and exchange.

Although in this system the man held the main part of the material and economic responsibilities within the family, the woman was no less accountable for its reputation: a physical and moral responsibility of which she was basically judged unworthy and incapable and which was at the root of her situation as a recluse.

So for both sexes, the unity, honour and survival of the family was regarded as prevailing over individual interests

2 The reality and the status of women in rural and bedouin Libya is noticeably different from that described here, particularly in the fact that the "infical" is difficult to apply there.

3 "The spaces, the times and the standards of female and male movement are defined very precisely," as D. Abrous says when talking about Algerian society in his doctoral thesis on "Honour in view of women working in Algeria", 1985.

and personal fulfilment. Thus marriage was mainly a family, tribal, economic and social affair, while conjugal relationships belonged to an extended family relationship (marriages between cousins were relatively frequent). The child represented an extension of the family and the tribe – and, in a way, the property of both. The single status was not accepted very well, particularly for women, but also for men.

In compensation for such weighty constraints on the individual, it must not be forgotten that for all the members of a family – men and women, of all ages – the family provided not only personal and social identity, but also the cohesion and security of the group on the economic and material as well as the personal and emotional level.

This traditional family order, going back thousands of years, does not seem to have developed much during the colonial and post-colonial period, despite the troubles that had occurred: the struggle against a colonising and Fascist Italy, the colonisation by an Italian population, the Second World War taking place partly across Libyan territory and followed by an international guardianship, with English occupation of Cyrenica, French occupation of Fezzan, and an Italian population being maintained in Tripolitania. It is true that women did participate, particularly in the fight for independence (cf. the story of Omar Mukhtar, the national hero of the uprising against the Italian colonisation), it took place mainly in the rural and bedouin environment; many women seen to have taken part directly in acts of war, even if their activities were often restricted to the traditional tasks reserved for the back-up troops, such as looking after the wounded.

We find, therefore, in 1951, when the country became independent, that the Libyan family had developed little in comparison to that of the preceding generations. Ch. Souriau, in her book *"The Economy of Women"* summarises the main characteristics of the traditional Libyan family in this way: the absence of men from the domestic area, which gave room for female relationships and practises, the mother-son relationship, the most important, prevented female society from forming itself into a "sex class", and also relegated to the background the relationship of the marital couple based on love (Western-style).

With independence, the emphasis on the Sunni[4] Arab-Moslem identity and a certain return to the traditions advocated by the monarchy were rather disadvantageous to hypothetical changes in the status of women. But, following the other Arab countries, the political leaders of the kingdom then decided to opt for a certain form of modernism. Thanks to oil (which they had started to develop around 1957) a large budget was allocated to education, regarded as one of the most suitable means for achieving this option[5]. Many schools were set up in the towns. The girls were going to benefit from this situation, of course. This access to education, and the modernisation which followed, were to be carried out within the strict limits of the traditions: the teaching could only take place in separate establishments and, for the girls, by women teachers. As could be expected, as soon as the girls reached puberty, they were taken back home, their knowledge rarely going beyond that of the primary level. Very few were given permission to continue their studies.

Moreover, in this generation, this quickly led to a big difference in the level of education between girls and boys. But things were slowly beginning to move on the women's side. The proof of that is that from 1955 they for once used the "infical" to their advantage: the first women's organisation appeared in Benghazi, then in 1957 in Tripoli, and then in other towns. The spirit may still have been far from "feminist", but they worked as catalysts for women to become aware of their own status.

The entry into modernity did not stop there. Around the 1960s, under various influences[6], a certain number of new laws were passed which were favourable to women[7]. The legal age of marriage for girls was fixed at 16 and women were

4 Sunni: following the "sunna", or tradition (as opposed to Shiism, a movement which contested the legality of the succession of the prophet Mohammed, and did not take long to develop its own dogma, while remaining a minority within the community of believers).

5 In this respect as in others, Libya was very behind its neighbours: in 1956, only 25 Moslem girls went to secondary schools, compared with 2,500 boys. Only the Faculty of Arts existed, with a grand total of 31 students.

6 The pressure of Arab, particularly Egyptian, feminist groups, started to make itself felt.

7 But, unlike Tunisia for example, they had not yet got as far as forming a "code of personal status".

given the right to choose their future husbands themselves, indeed in certain cases to apply for divorce. Furthermore, although very few of them had exercised a profession outside the family home, discrimination in salaries between men and women was ended. A little later, in 1963, after making education compulsory until the end of primary school, Libyan women were even given the right to vote and take part in politics.

For more than 90% of the female population these laws remained theoretical, as in practice the patriarchal tradition continued to impose itself. But also at this time a number of Libyans in the towns started to adopt Western lifestyles, particularly under the influence of the English and Italians, of whom there were still many in the country. In this restricted urban environment, some women were already daring to give up the traditional costume and the veil (hijab), but for all that they still did not take part in political life.

The first association of a really feminist nature, which appeared in 1965, immediately set up a magazine specifically for women[8]. Its members more or less openly rejected the limits that society had until then assigned to them. At that time, whenever a woman left her private space for the public area, it still represented an attempt to go beyond, it questioned her identity as an "honest" woman. The transgression of the existing cultural order was still felt as a threat against the stability of the relationships of the sexes and as upsetting the relations of traditional power recognised between men and women.

However that may be, at the time when the "free officers" took power, quite a significant number of Libyan women (around 10,000 to 15,000) had attained a higher level of education.

Although power was taken – from El Beida to Benghazi and Tripoli – without women, they showed interest and support for the new authorities from the beginning. When, in September 1969, the team of "free officers" addressed all

8 The first of its kind in North Africa, this magazine has continued to exist under different names but without interruption until now. Today it is called *El Intalaqa (Divorce)*.

Col. Ghadafi with feminine supporters

the citizens, men and women, to announce important social changes and declare equal rights for all, calling explicitly on women, the latter put themselves right in the front row to listen to these new voices. The images of the very start of the revolution already show that women were present at public demonstrations in large and unusual numbers.

The slogans of the official speech had a new emphasis: "Liberty", "Socialism", and "Unity". It was particularly the first term, expressed as "the need of the individual to free himself from the oppression of past centuries and to emancipate himself from humiliation, injustice and ignorance[9], which immediately struck a chord in women, who inter-

9 Speech of 7.9.1969.

Ghadafi addressing a Women's Union Meeting

preted it for themselves, recognised in the ideology presented their own aspirations for a real personal and social identity.

A few months later, in 1970, when for the first time in the history of Libya all women without discrimination were invited to come and discuss their needs and their desires with the new authorities in a congress specially organised for them, many of them responded to this call, hurrying from all areas of the country despite traditional and family con- straints. As a result of this historic meeting, which was followed by many others, a series of laws was adopted in accordance with the motions and resolutions of the meeting in a sense which was favourable to women.

The new team continued to recognise education as an important instrument for achieving cultural transformations and as a main resource for the social advancement of women. But achieving real access for women to educational institutions was not going to happen just like that, as the experience of the predecessors had shown. A considerable gap had arisen between the educational level of the two sexes within this first educated generation, a gap which was at the origin of the increasing number of marriages to foreign women, which a law supposed to protect Libyan women was later going to almost prohibit.

Ghadafi and his team made it a priority to tackle this problem of the educational discrepancy. From then on they were careful to have no more discrimination in education, which in a country with such a disparate population (geographical, economic and social) was not a simple task at the beginning.

The school-leaving age was raised to 16 – and, in parallel, that of marriage to 18[10]. Educational establishments at all levels were built in the secondary towns – and even, for primary education, in the rural districts, including the oases. They also started to encourage co-education (at the primary school level, as the universities had been mixed from the time they were set up). And, to be more efficient, they were finally going to take sanctions against parents who refused education for their daughters after the age of puberty. Later, they would oblige girls of this age to exchange the "farashia" for the "battledress" for their participation in military training. Finally, they would ensure that the award of study grants would not allow any injustice of a sexist nature.

These measures led to interesting results. These are shown in the table below, which reveals that the percentage of girls taking part in education not only rose from year to year, but also increased twice as quickly as the percentage of boys during this twelve year-period.

They were not going to stop there. Many other measures were taken which show the Libyan leaders' concern to encourage the improvement of women's living conditions in many ways.

From 1972, the old and new women's associations had

10 At present the legal age for marriage is fixed at 20 for both sexes.

Number of male and female students in two school years

Education:	1969–1970		1982–1983		Average annual increase	
	Boys	Girls	Boys	Girls	Boys	Girls
Primary........................	214,100	110,500	379,700	342,000	4.5	9.1
Preparatory	31,700	6,500	132,400	96,500	11.6	23.1
General secondary............	7,700	1,400	40,000	18,900	13.5	22.2
Technical secondary..........	1,500	–	16,500	4,900	20.2	–
Teacher training colleges						
Teachers	3,000	1,700	10,800	19,900	10.3	20.8
University and higher........	3,700	400	22,700	7,200	15.0	24.9
Total	261,700	120,500	602,100	489,400	6.6	11.4

been grouped into a national federation, but without great development of their activity programmes. It was only three years later, in 1975, under the encouragement of Ghadafi himself, that the Union of Libyan Women[11] was formed, with the sworn aim of directly fighting against the abuses of the patriarchal society.

While the new organisation was going to open branches in all the provinces, the Tripoli head office was given a generous budget and received a large building equipped to provide courses. It is said that the Colonel personally saw to it that the persons appointed to be in charge came up to the ambitions of the regime. The first generation of directors and tutors was selected, taught and trained in Libya. Many varied activities emerged: activities in the educational field, catching up on school first, then professional training, secretarial apprenticeships, sewing etc, but also courses in political training.

In parallel, dispensaries and medico-social centres were set up to help mothers-to-be, for child care, and even family planning (which demonstrated, at the time, in view of the fact that it was an under-populated country, quite an openness of mind). Day-care centres were experimented with[12] to relieve the tasks of women who found themselves in difficult situations (widows, divorcees, girls or women who were cut off from their families and were forced to earn their living.

In the rural areas, the Ghadafian regime put the emphasis on social progress in relation to the development of

11 Ittihad Nisa'i Libya.
12 Despite the precepts of the *Green Book* (quoted p. 47).

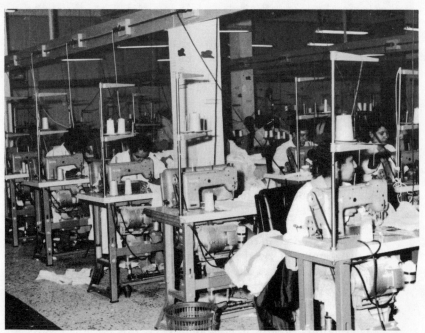

Clothes Factory

Electronic Transmissions

agriculture. Rural action centres had training programmes reserved for uneducated women and girls, including, as well as literacy, lessons on housekeeping, child-care and hygiene, as well as technical programmes[13]. Lasting for four hours a day for six months, these training courses were soon made compulsory, despite the sometimes vigorous opposition of the husbands (even though collective transport and child-minding was organised for the women).

The managers of these centres were trained on the job, thanks to a specific action of the Secretariat (Ministry) of Agriculture. But for all these actions the Libyan officials were quite largely inspired by American concepts and experiences which the first managers trained for the social service had studied in the United States. We should note that this programme of social advancement developed throughout Libya just as much to the advantage of men as women.

However, these measures affirmed the dominant pre-occupations of the Libyan leaders in favour of transforming the living conditions of women. Thus the development of legislative theory and practice date from this period. From the patriarchal concept which was very protective of women and children[14] it came gradually to express the emancipatory wish proclaimed by the *Green Book*.

It is indeed true that the principles of defending the family and giving priority to children were maintained as the basis of society[15]. But the resistance and criticism did not take long to appear, as the patriarchy was still alive and well.

13 These included driving lessons – for cars and tractors – the rudiments of small-scale animal husbandry, bee-keeping, veterinary medicine, notions on the storage of food products (e.g. freezing) etc.

14 In the event of divorce, the woman keeps the house. She is also given custody of the children. If the woman works outside the home, she has to prove she can meet her maternal obligations and be given permission to feed her child during working hours. Nobody has the right to set tasks on women which are too heavy physically, they are not allowed to do night work. A mother-to-be is entitled to 8 weeks' maternity leave.

15 A healthy and happy society, according to the official speech, is a society in which the individual develops naturally within his family. In this basic cell the child must, at least in the initial years, be brought up by his mother, on whom he is completely dependent: "The child must be brought up in the family where mother-hood, fatherhood and brotherhood prevail, and not in an institution which is like a poultry farm", declares the *Green Book*. Also: Societies in which the existence and the unity of the family are put at jeopardy, whatever the circumstances, are like those fields whose flora is threatened by erosion, fire or drought". *Green Book* 1984 ed.

Whether this was an argumentative strategy or his own conviction, the Colonel's speech had remained careful, narrowly sticking to traditions and customs, placing women in their maternal role and referring repeatedly to religion to guide girls more towards professions which were defined as feminine.

But this speech was soon going to become more progressive, indeed positively provocative. It seems that the change in tone and also content can only be explained by the fact of Ghadafi and his team observing failure, that is the liberation of women had not yet happened, and neither the effort at education, nor the amendment of the legislation, nor the creation of favourable objective conditions, had had a real effect on relationships between men and women. These relationships remained practically unchanged, even if a certain number of women were timidly starting to assist at the basic congresses (where places were reserved for them on the front row) and a few dared to speak up. The integration of women into social and political life continued to be part of the theoretical domain, if not Utopia. The patriarchate remained the dominant ideology and practices remained on the whole sexist.

This observation led to research on other methods of achieving an egalitarian society. It was becoming obvious that they had to attack mentalities, not just institutions, and try to make them develop by other means[16].

It was first of all by civic and political education and the spread of the new ideology contained in the *Green Book*,

16 The Libyan leader's awareness of the necessity to go further than the legislative reforms was rather ahead of the spirit of the times. It was in 1987, for example, at a Unesco conference in her country, that Queen Nour of Jordan declared herself to be on the same track: "The particular challenge in the Arab World was more complex than simply offering men and women equal opportunities of education, employment, advancement and social benefits. It was the challenge of fusing the contemporary quest for equality of opportunity with the powerful instincts of an ancient social heritage that had traditionally defined a woman's public role in a highly restricted manner, in favour of her domestic role as wife and mother . . . " It is also interesting to remember that even in Europe the spirit of the legislation remained steadfastly patriarchal. It was only in 1965 that a French wife was able to work outside her home in accordance with her own decision and without permission from her husband (Art. 223 Civil Code). During the same period in Holland, which is however renowned for its feminist spirit, a woman needed permission from her father to marry until the age of thirty. In France it was only a few years ago that the concept of the husband as the "head of the family" was abandoned.

which it became compulsory to study in all the teaching establishments. Then it was by public speeches or talks on occasions of direct contact with limited groups of the population (for example parents of pupils, soldiers etc) or through television. In other words, a systematic effort at indoctrination was launched.

For this Ghadafi enlisted the help of the members of the Revolutionary Committees, which movement had been started a short while before. On the women's side, the "Female Revolutionary Movement" (which was later to be integrated into the Revolutionary Committees) was launched in 1978. About a hundred women, taken from among those most progressive and open to the ideas of the regime, received special training designed to turn them into the advocates and cantors of the new ideology. Their mission was to overcome the resistances of the women themselves, to lead them to "truly liberate" themselves.

Then a new period started in the course of the emancipation of Libyan women[17]. From 1979 new models were presented: first that of the "woman at arms", then that of the "revolutionary nun". The Women's Military Academy, established a short time before, very quickly became the symbol of the emergence of the new female élites.

It would not take long for these new models[18] to go far beyond the formal concepts of the *Green Book*, certain precepts of which were, moreover, not even defended any more[19].

The equation woman = wife and mother was abandoned. A war was openly declared on patriarchal ideology and reality.

17 This new period had, in reality, already been started in 1977 with the transformation of Libyan society into the "Jamahirya".
18 See Part II Chapter IV.
19 For example the obligation of women to reproduce.

Mothers of families doing voluntary military training.

Chapter IV

From reproduction to production
Ideology and economic realities

Whether the inspiration had come to him as a heritage of such a fertile and varied past, or whether it expressed the resources of a personal doctrine, the Ghadafian concept of feminism and equality of the sexes takes on the appearance of a theory based on the following axioms and postulates:

1. A man and a woman are different, one is not the other;
2. Equality must be understood more in terms of "equity", it is an ethical equality.
3. The Jamahirya must distance itself from the West and the East, as the concept of women in both these civilisations is erroneous, the West – capitalist or Marxist – hardly taking its female nature into account any more and demanding that women behave like men, whereas the East only wants to see them as a reproductive force;
4. The feminist ideology proposed by the *Green Book*, like most of the theories that it professes, is not presented as a

Libyan or Arab or Islamic concept, it claims to be universal[1].

In the Libya of today, equality is declared to be an aim in itself, not an instrument in the service of the economy. But what sort of equality is it exactly?

In one of his many declarations, the Leader of the revolution proclaimed: "In the new Jamahiryan society, each man and woman citizen will have his equal place". Is this a Utopia eclipsing social contradictions and economic realities? It does seem, at this stage, that it is not an equality of identity, but an equality in difference. The great chance in Ghadafian egalitarianism lies in its ability to cling or not to the reality that it is supposed to model. If the ideology goes too far from the social infrastructure, from the civic maturity, from the degree of cohesion of the group, straight away the gap risks turning into violence or a social explosion. The Libyan leader, despite the radicalism with which he presents and defends the values of his ideology, seems to be careful, without always managing to succeed however[2], to avoid these risks. In him we see a political realism contrasting with his ideological radicalism.

Mentalities in old-fashioned Libyan society had for centuries been developing in the opposite direction to the concept of equality. It was foreseeable that resistance would be in proportion to the gap between old and new concepts[3]. It is in this context that the sometimes contradictory double-talk must be understood and explained. We do find alternately ideological and Utopian talk – referring to only the revolutionary values – and realistic and pragmatic talk – referring to the economy and the necessities of develop-

1 In a speech made on East German radio in 1982, Colonel Ghadafi addressed all women, Eastern as well as Western, to encourage them to produce a real world revolution, and to win back their place in society by banishing injustice and recovering their dignity and their liberty.

2 Cf. open conflict between soldiers and "militia"; muted struggles or real fights between Popular Committees and Revolutionary Committees; intellectual confrontations between technocrats and ideologists etc.

3 Despite the precautions taken, several of the Leader's proposals to the People's General Congress (new law on divorce, compulsory training of women) were rejected. Cf. the notorious General Congress of "the Three Nos" (1984). It is striking to note that this General Congress was made up almost entirely of men.

ment. Ghadafi seems to have wanted to answer the reticence of his compatriots in advance, reticence based both on the apathy of certain strata of the population and what the traditionalists could denounce as an attack on the values of all time, particularly a weakening of the family. By making a kind of higher bid on identity, Ghadafi sought to warn an opposition which he was expecting in advance.

So, especially at the beginning, the emphasis was put on the natural separation of the roles resulting from the fact that nature had created man and woman differently (women produce).

This "biological" stance could seem to be a new justification of the patriarchy. To deny women as a social category did not imply a priori that the system of the "infical" was being rejected, nor that domination of one sex by the other was being abandoned. But the "biological" orientation was to nurture more than one misunderstanding[4].

To understand this position properly, the content of the ideology must be analysed. Its aim was in no way to consolidate the patriarchy, and the declaration which is significant in this respect is at the start of the chapter on women in the *Green Book*: "A woman is first of all a human being . . . then a female just as a man is a male". This was a truly provocative idea as it was formally opposed to the patriarchal vision. Women, for the first time in Libya, were defined first of all as social beings, not as biological beings. Suddenly they found themselves in a position of equality, at least in principle, with men, and from this it followed that their relationship which had previously been reduced to the biological relationship, became a social relationship.

This relationship did indeed keep as its primary function the organisation of reproduction of individuals; but from then on this was defined as a social act. The dimension of the individual desires (of both sexes) would prevail over biolo-

4 Thus, at a meeting between Colonel Ghadafi and the Egyptian Women's Union in Cairo in 1972, Ghadafi was literally booed by his Egyptian feminist audience because the Head of the Revolution's arguments were not well perceived. Jihane Saadat, the widow of the Egyptian President, brings this event up in her autobiography. She uses it improperly to make it appear that things were still like that in the Libya of 1987.

gical "fate"; the double decision (that of both partners) would win over female nature, which implied the possible logic of rejecting motherhood. So the woman, still the main person responsible for reproduction of the species, was no longer destined to be a mother solely by force of nature; motherhood was no longer endured but chosen.

In line with this new way of looking at things, the male category, presented until then as a general category to which all women and men should refer, became, like the female category, a particular case. Consequently, Ghadafi was going to have to join up the field of production and the field of reproduction, particularly by decreeing that motherhood and work at home were "other forms of production". From then on a child would be regarded in Libya as an internal product of the very first class, an investment thought of as essentially productive"[5]. Work in the home would be rehabilitated as a real job. With these fundamentally new stands, Ghadafi established women (on an equal level to men) in their status as responsible citizens, but also as a working force.

This particular and modernist concept[6] of women's work means that there would no longer be a difference between work at home and an outside job. The latter would no longer be regarded as granting women real liberty and emancipation. It would later receive a certain recognition as a means of self-affirmation and personal fulfilment[7]. However, the work myth which is so widespread elsewhere would never be mentioned here[8]. On the other hand, participation by

5 Ch. Souriau, op. cit.

6 To abstract the work of women (motherhood and domestic tasks) from the fact of their being invisible is one of today's problems for which a solution has not been found as yet in any country.

7 "The question is not to know whether a woman must work or not . . . Society must provide work for all its valid members – men and women – who need it on condition that each individual can exercise his activity in the area that suits him . . . Liberty is that each human being acquires the recognition which allows him to exercise the activity which suits him". (*Green Book* p. 93 Ed. Green Book Research Centre, Tripoli 1984).

8 Z. Zohri and S. Azzi in *The economic and social role of women in social dynamics* (Ed. of Green Book Research Centre 1983), reiterating the official statements, write: "It is not because in some countries the percentage of working women is higher that women there are more liberated or more emancipated". With regard to the statistics, they emphasise: "Neither the counts of women among the working forces, nor the income that they earn, provide us with information about the quality of relationships between men and women".

women in all political and social instances of society would be strongly encouraged, indeed helped by measures of a practical nature[9].

This rehabilitation of the role of women in the home, a real revaluation of their social status by ideology, was it comparable with the realities and the constraints of a country rich in oil but weak in working forces? It had the obvious effect of keeping the Libyan woman outside the real productive circuit: a "luxury" that Libya could no longer afford on the day following the second oil shock, which was going to reduce its foreign currency income by two-thirds.

Was this a chance coincidence or clever planning? We note that several measures were taken which seemed contradictory to the aim of improving women's living conditions.

Under the pretext of putting the Libyans to work, and increasing the country's productivity with the after-oil period in mind, small private businesses were closed (accused of being socially parasitic), foreigners were expelled in huge numbers (said to cost too much foreign currency), the facilities of a service economy were abolished (services often run, furthermore, by Tunisians and Moroccans).

The effect of these measures was that women became the first victims. Ghadafi, aware of that, was not at all troubled and declared almost cynically: "If women want to eat cakes, they have only to make them at home; as for hairdressers, they are very capable of doing their hair by themselves". A little later, he went even further by speaking of the possibility of having children taught at home by their mothers for the first year of primary education.

By replacing the foreign workers by Libyan women, it is clear that here there is a first attempt to shift a certain number of jobs from the "outside" to the "inside", and thus increase the productivity of women, while avoiding the disintegration of the family and keeping away the classic patriarchal critics.

As for the results of these measures, it is hardly possible to quantify them, even approximately. However, we have been able to make several observations: the hairdressing salons were from then on run by their Libyan owners; cakes

9 Arrangement of working hours, on-site crèches etc.

and other articles for domestic consumption were made at home, and sometimes sold in the area (for example for weddings); cleaning and laundry services were organised on a neighbourhood scale, at the initiative of women.

Semi-success or semi-failure – after these changes "Brother Moammar" even so lost a little of his popularity among women[10] – still a few years later many "services" were again taken over by the Arab neighbours (returning Moroccans, then Tunisians, in the fluctuating context of North African co-operation).

Meanwhile the speech on women had itself changed: the merits of "enriching" work for women (in the sense of personal fulfilment) were recognised. What is more, celibacy was, if not encouraged, at least tolerated.

These latter developments, it seemed to us, took place at least partly under the direct pressure of women. Whatever the case, such a development shows the intimate interweaving of interests (economic, political and social) belonging to the category or the group and the influence exercised constantly by the whole of society on these elements, and vice versa.

Although the ideological vision has remained unchanged in fact, at least the tactics employed to achieve the objectives were varied, if not even contradictory. The status of Libyan women, it is undeniable, has been profoundly reshaped; but her place in society remains daily renegotiable and subject to interpretation.

How is this new situation lived by the Libyan women themselves? And by the males around them? This double question is the subject of the second part of the work, dedicated to on-site research.

---

10 Cf. the wife of a regime official exclaimed: "I'm fed up with always being treated as a guinea-pig".

PART TWO

THE WOMEN'S MILITARY ACADEMY AND THE NEW FEMALE ÉLITES

However far back in history we go, men are confronted with the image of the "warrior male". In the same way, motherhood has always been the distinctive feature of women; "women give life and men protect it."

History is rich, however, in examples of exceptions to this rule. From ancient antiquity, we find groups of armed women who have made war their specific activity – the Amazons, the Dahomey warriors in the XIXth century, or again those legendary women of whom there are countless examples in the history of ancient Libya.

Without going back several thousands of years to the remains whose elegant (although often war-like) silhouettes adorn the rocky sites of Fezzan's barren heights, the search for a superior female archetype bears many fruits across the rich past of Hellenic and Roman Libya – from the Cyrenian Nymph[1] to Pentapole Berenice, daughter of Magas, King of Cyrene[2], and Medusa of Leptis Magna[3]. But without doubt the best place to stop to pay homage and refer, and to try and find the sources of a mythical "mulier libyca" at arms, is at the haughty figure of Queen Dahya ben Talit el Kahena. It is this queen, who ruled over a Judaized Berber tribe originat-

[1] Her statue, erected everywhere by the Greeks, exalted the legend of she who "despised the plying back and forth and who, sword in hand, conquered the lions to ensure a happy peace for her father's flocks".

[2] Because a lock of her hair, which she had dedicated to the goddess Aphrodite so that her husband, Ptolemeus III would come back safe and sound from an expedition to Syria, had disappeared from the temple where it had been put, the astronomer Conon of Samos declared that her hair had been turned into stars, and he gave the constellation the name of "Berenice's Hair" (3rd century B.C.).

[3] One of the "Gorgons" with hair of snakes, who at a single glance turned enemies into stone. She was "reinvented" by the Romans, who adorned the Leptis Magna forum with her (3rd century A.D.).

ing from Tripolitania, the Djeraoua, to whom Ibn Khaldoun, in his *History of the Berbers*, attributes organisation of the resistance to the invader in the Aures, the first Arab-Moslem invasion.

But there is another character whom we should be careful not to leave out, as she is known to every Moslem man and woman. She is Aicha, the daughter of Abou Bakr and favourite wife of Mohammed, who, after playing an important political role during the Prophet's lifetime, distinguished herself on the death of her husband by raising an army and fighting at its head against the man whom she thought unworthy of succeeding the Prophet – Ali Abu Talib[4].

Was the Leader of the Libyan revolution inspired by this illustrious example? Or, more prosaically, did Colonel Ghadafi think that a strict observance of the "infical", at least at the start, was necessary, and that women officers should be trained up to give military instruction to the schoolgirls? Whatever the case, the formation of a military academy especially for women seemed necessary to him, in 1979, within the context of a global strategy. This "necessity", moreover, is more easily understood if we remember that the concept of the militarisation of women had emerged in 1975, as a natural consequence of the formation of the people's army, and by application of the egalitarian ideology, which is the axiom on which the participation of women in the life of the nation is based.

So from that time, the Colonel had emphasised that the nature of war had changed; it was no longer just a confrontation of warrior men, but a general conflagration which ignored any distinction between front and rear, between soldiers and civilians, between men and women.

Referring mainly to the events in the Middle East (Palestine and Lebanon), Ghadafi had already advocated the "necessity" of giving women the means to defend themselves[5]. It thus seemed natural to him that a military

---

4 This battle, known as "The Camel Battle" was the start of Shiism.

5 On this subject we can mention, among other initiatives, those of the many Palestinian women, also of a group of Lebanese Christian women (who, through conviction, committed themselves as an armed group under the banner of the Lebanese Forces).

Gorgon, Leptis Magna

Bérénice, Leptis Magna

Ghadafi visiting the Women's Military Adademy

training institution especially for women should be set up in Libya[6]. And, straight away, this innovation claimed to be both a "model" and an instrument at the service of the Arab world. As a result, it was opened up to students from other Arab "regions". Today roughly ten per cent of its students are non-Libyans (Lebanese, Palestinian, Sudanese, Syrian etc).

A tool for technical training, the Women's Military Academy (WMA) was also a tool for political and ideological instruction for women. It was rapidly going to represent the most active "jewel" of Ghadafian feminism, and it was mainly from this point of view that the Academy seemed

6 In the same year a military high school for girls only was opened in Benghazi.

to merit particular study. For although the foundation of the WMA seems to respond first to a military imperative, it is clear that from the moment it was conceived the institution had other ambitions. In reality it was to provoke, shock, and create a precedent, to directly attack out-of-date mentalities.

From the moment when the WMA was opened on 2 February 1979, Ghadafi presented his programme as follows: "Women will only be free and respected and exercise all their rights when they are strong and possess all the weapons: weapons of fire as well as weapons of science, awareness, culture and revolution. We will take a strategic step, a qualitative leap, if women enter the army". Straight away he defined it more precisely: "The WMA only concerns a limited number of girls, as not all are suitable to become officers. These girls must meet the health requirements, have personality, be cultivated. A diploma, even from a university, is not enough, a woman soldier or officer will be judged on her personality, her competence and her general culture, with these she will succeed in joining men and soldiers. From there she will be able to attain military honour, be at the forefront of the 'people at arms', and set an example to all women".

It was in 1983 that we were allowed, for the first time, to enter that particularly well-guarded precinct that is the Tripoli Women's Academy. Built on a huge site on the edge of the coast, near to the centre of the capital, the establishment is surrounded by a high wall, the monotony broken only by the double gates at the entrance. Viewed from the outside, this property reminded us more of a prison institution than an educational establishment for girls. In 1991 the entrance was modified and the building looks much better now. But once we had passed through the forbidding surround, the welcome we received was a happy contrast. The serious look displayed by a colonel-director (doubtless appropriate) was contradicted by the smiling, friendly attitude of the other members of the "staff", largely female. In accordance with tradition, flowers were very quickly offered, followed by the tea ceremony. An introduction of all the staff by the colonel was followed by a detailed visit to the buildings and exercise grounds. To finish, we were taken to the "Golden Book", displaying the very recent signature of Mrs Indira Gandhi, which was obviously a source of pride for the Management and all the students.

This first contact, friendly and open, greatly encouraged us, in this symbolic and almost mythical institution of the Jamahirya, to undertake an investigation the very principle of which could, at the start, be regarded as a quest for the impossible. So many "indiscreet" questions rushed into our minds! How did the establishment run on a day-to-day basis? Where did the students come from? And the staff? Who were, in truth, these smiling, welcoming girls? Why had they chosen a military career? And how was such an experience lived, at first glance one so far removed from the traditions and lifestyles of Libyan society?

Later (over a period of three years), through numerous discussions with the members of the staff and particularly thanks to the in-depth interviews which we were authorised to conduct with about twenty student officers and officers, we were going to obtain most of the answers we wanted to all these questions.

Chapter I

The Women's Military Academy as a military institution

Study cycles and levels of training

The WMA, where the students are all boarders, provides teaching on two levels:

– It trains women soldiers in three months, from the end of the fourth year of secondary school,

– It trains women officers in two years, from the "bac" (higher school-leaving certificate).

The total capacity of the Academy is 1,000 students, but this number has never been reached to date[1]. The numbers are fixed each year by the army depending on its requirements, not by the management of the WMA.

For both training levels, the *study programmes* are largely the same as those of the other military academies. There are two exceptions, however – the number of specialisations

---

1 Between 1980 and 1988 the numbers varied, for the soldiers between 170 and 410 students per session, and for the officers between 80 and 210 per year. We can estimate that since its foundation the WMA has in ten years trained roughly 1,600 officers, and roughly four times as many soldiers.

Classroom

offered to women officers, and some physical exercises which are deemed too hard for them.

As well as the general training, the *soldiers' training* programme includes the following subjects: morse, ciphers, shorthand and typing, first aid, and military music[2].

The WMA also offers its student soldiers the opportunity to prepare for the "bac" on site, and thus to follow on with officer training: 10 to 15% use this opportunity. After obtaining the diploma, most are assigned as officers to give military training to girls at secondary school.

In the first year of studies, the *officer training* consists of

2 The women's orchestra, of good quality, takes students specialised in an instrument.

basic theoretical instruction relating to various military subjects[3]. For the second year, the students are divided into four specialised sections – communications, electronics, land-land and land-air defence, and administration.

The mornings are generally taken up with outdoor exercises (handling weapons, group development). Several times a year, manoeuvres take place outside Tripoli lasting for 10 to 15 days, sometimes the manoeuvres are combined with the two men's training academies (MMA). The training year, divided into two parts of 5 months each, is broken up by the examinations and the holidays. During their time at the WMA it is possible for the student officers to, at the same time, enrol in a university faculty. Roughly twenty percent of the total number take advantage of this opportunity.

Buildings and equipment

The Academy is fitted out comfortably – single rooms, in principle reserved for the "staff" (but, each semester, the management also makes a few single rooms available to the best students as a reward for their good results), spacious dormitories, with numerous washrooms and well equipped, for the students (who each have their own table and wardrobe).

As well as the teaching rooms, the WMA has a modern laboratory, and, outside, huge areas for the manoeuvres and exercises, as well as several sports grounds. Meals are eaten together (collective restaurant). There is also a library, a leisure and games room, and a self-service type shop, which give the students some recreational facilities on site.

1. DISCUSSIONS WITH THE STAFF AT THE WMA

Selection and organisation

To present the method and the objectives of the training given, we will let the colonel-director of the Academy speak. We naturally had repeated and varied conversations with him. The interview which follows summarises the main points of our discussions.

---

3 Geography and history of the army, cartography and photography, chemistry, military tactics, security, army psychology, international law and office work.

Transmission exercises

Handling of Arms

Practice loading of a fixed cannon

Training with a light tank

How are the candidates for the WMA selected?

"A selection committee, consisting of several men and women officers, judges the candidates both according to their school marks and their behaviour. A certificate of morality, usually issued by the Popular Committee of the neighbourhood or the village of origin, is also required. Finally, an open interview takes place with the candidate about her motives, her aspirations, and her understanding of the Revolution. If she is selected, she will then undergo a medical examination".

What are the aims that the WMA is pursuing with this recruitment?

"The defence of the country is the responsibility of all the citizens, men and women, that's the basic principle. But for women to participate, they first had to be liberated from their burdens, from their social constraints, and given the same degree of freedom as men.

By promoting the introduction of women into active life, in a sector which is so removed from tradition, the WMA aims in particular to put them on an equal footing with men, and to guarantee them the resources to defend their liberty as well as their native land".

What was recruitment like at the beginning?
Was there much resistance from the families?

"Since it was something completely new, and despite the fact that the population had already for two years been used to seeing girls in uniform because of the military training in the schools and high schools, the families began by refusing to let their daughters enter the WMA. But, after many many discussions, explanations and confrontations, most understood and accepted, so much so that today the problem posed by the hostility of the families practically no longer exists. Entering the WMA has almost become something commonplace.

Before the lessons began, the first year, we had started a presentation campaign in the high schools. The Leader himself had explained the objectives of the WMA in several talks, and called on the young women to enrol. We had to demonstrate flexibility and adaptability.

91

At the beginning we could not demand the 'bac' for the selection of the student officers, and we recruited at final or pre-final year level. But that first year group had the opportunity to prepare for the 'bac' here. Since then, those who already have it when they come are encouraged, in accordance with the Leader's directives, to enrol in one of the faculties of Tripoli university".

How was the "staff" of the establishment formed?

"At the beginning, we didn't have enough women soldiers who were adequately trained, so the majority of the staff was male. Now it's the opposite – we have a majority of women. The current training personnel is made up of 30 women and only 5 men.

Today, the military subjects proper are still taught by men, as we do not have enough specialised women. The civil subjects, however, are taught by lecturers, men and women, from the University. In total the internal and external training staff consists of 150 people, including 4 doctors and 12 nurses."

Is the training given by the WMA different from that of the MMAs, and in what way?

"The basic training for an officer, in all cases, is two years. The first year is exactly the same in the MMA or the WMA, except for some physical exercises. For the second year, the specialisation year, the choice is more limited at the WMA – 4 special sectors instead of 6 at the MMA. So, at the WMA there aren't any specialisations requiring a certain physical strength, such as driving tanks. Likewise, the choice of weapons used is adapted to the women's physical ability – only light or medium weapons are used, but this also applies to some of the men.

During the second year, joint exercises take place between the two academies. It is obvious that the future officers will have to get used to the teams being mixed if we want women to take part in combat alongside men.

Another difference is that the men's academies have, for a year now, written a third year of technical specialisation into their programme. This special section will probably be opened up to women in a year or two.

In 1987 a new military administration institute was opened. This was immediately accessible to women, as are, moreover, all the higher institutes of aviation, marine etc. Several women are already training as war pilots. And our national civil aviation company also employs one woman pilot.

In short, if you really wanted to make a distinction, a subtle difference between the training given by the WMA and the MMA, I would say that the women's is a little more intellectual than the others, as in the latter the students are not allowed to follow courses at the University".

In many countries, particularly in France, women soldiers do not have the right to take part in "close combat". What is the Libyan attitude on this subject?

"Whether officers or soldiers, the female Libyan military are authorised to take part, but they are not forced to. As an example, I can tell you that four women went as volunteers to take part in the war in Tchad. Our principle is to refuse them nothing, to let them make their decisions themselves. For example, if a woman really wants to enrol in a physically difficult section or take part in certain exercises which are not required, she is allowed to. We do not want to prevent or exclude them. It's the same thing for those who failed the medical exam, they are given their chance to try in spite of everything. But generally they quickly realise their limits.

Apart from these cases, no more than 3 to 4% of the students give up the WMA training during their studies, and when that happens it is for personal, social or health reasons."

Is there an obligation for the students to observe prayers?

"No, we are by principle against any form of obligation. It is up to them to decide. They must be responsible for themselves, and if they are given ten minutes five times a day to pray, they are free to do so or not. There is no checking. It's up to their own personal conscientiousness. But I think, however, that most of them say their prayers more or less regularly".

Once they have obtained the diploma, how are the students posted? Don't you again come across problems with the families?

"There is an army assignment committee. This takes great account of the student's choice, and particularly where they come from. So as a priority they always try to assign candidates to the town where their family comes from so that they can reintegrate into their family environment. The same is done, moreover, for the men, as family support and solidarity are very important and must be maintained and encouraged as much as possible. This is one of the principles in the *Green Book*: 'It is natural to stay close to one's family'.

But if this isn't possible, they discuss the best solution with the student. It's up to her to understand that she also has her duty as a patriot and a revolutionary.

The parents pose hardly any problems here either. From the time when the family accepted the general objectives of the WMA, it is led automatically to agree to the daughter's posting in the army. There is one case, however, when the civil state comes into play – when the woman soldier is married. Then she is usually orientated towards an office job. But that's sometimes the reason why girls don't want – at least not straight away – to get married!".

And the army itself, is it satisfied with the female element?

"Yes, on the whole the army seems satisfied with the training given to the women military. We can say overall that there are no particular criticisms. Women have often even shown themselves to be better than men for certain tasks.

It is true that over the years we have made several amendments to the programmes. We are always trying to improve the training in line with requirements".

What about the male soldiers, have they not felt it to be competition, as has sometimes been the case in other countries?

"Here, truly not. We have not felt this competition. The third theory – the *Green Book* – is accepted by everybody, and gives the same place to men as to women, equal place and power for all.

They will gladly give up their place to a woman. So, I will probably give up mine here to a woman[4]. That's normal, it's the logical consequence of having agreed to look after the training of women. Today, any woman must be able to get to the same functions as a man, including, isn't that right, the highest – that of the Leader!"

* *
*

We had an interview with one of the doctors in the Academy on the health conditions there and the supervision of the physical and mental condition of the staff. The information obtained complements the picture of the WMA given by the director.

Dr F, who was of Egyptian nationality and had been at the WMA for 4 years, was one of the 4 doctors (2 of whom were women) who made up the permanent health team which was assisted by 12 nurses (6 of whom were Libyans).

– The hospital set up in the WMA has 20 beds (only 6 were occupied at the time of the interview). Clients from outside (military personnel) are also treated there. Only minor surgical operations can be carried out (there is no anaesthetic on the site).

– According to Dr F, the state of health of both the students and the training staff is very good. He added: "Women are more resistant, and in particular more motivated, than men". Here they treat minor accidents (shock, contusions), on-going menstrual problems, and ordinary questions of general medicine. There are few psychosomatic illnesses, according to Dr F. For more serious things, although these are rare, the patient is evacuated to the central military hospital.

– Although the women military have a lighter training programme than the men, they even so have a considerable physical effort to make. For example, they go on night marches 15 km long carrying their weapons, without stopping. A doctor follows in a car. Likewise, a doctor is present at the outdoor exercises.

– They are closely watched from a medical and also

4 Since 1987, the position of assistant to the director (rank of captain) has been held by a woman.

mental point of view (to avoid "accidents" in relationships between women as between women and men; "If two girls look too intimate, we separate them, but not without first talking to them").

– Sometimes, when they first come to the WMA, there are students who find it difficult to cope with the regime of 6 hours' sleep. Generally they get used to it quite quickly, they can also have a nap to catch up with the required amount of sleep.

– Only 3 to 4% cannot cope physically with the regime. We warn them at the medical exam, but still we give them the chance to try. They themselves have to take the decision as to whether they give up or not. We always encourage them, in the medical field as in all the others, to accept their own responsibilities. That is a principle of the WMA.

These two interviews gave us a sort of official picture of the WMA. But what were things like from the students' point of view? What did they say about life at the Academy? And to start with, who were they?

2. DISCUSSIONS WITH THE STUDENT OFFICERS

A brief written questionnaire, relating to data of a general nature, was distributed to all the student officers of the WMA in order to determine the representativeness of our sample. The following information which came out of its analysis gives a better outline of the students.

– Their age varied between 17 and 26 (for the majority between 18 and 22). One-third of them had entered the WMA before taking the "bac", which they then continued to prepare for, and took it there the same year.

– As for their geographical origins, the student officers of the WMA came from all areas of the Jamahirya. Roughly one-third were natives of the town of Tripoli.

That year, among all the students, 12% were non-Libyans (from Lebanon, Syria and Sudan).

– As to social origin, the majority of the students came from large families (5 to 12 children), and from very different

backgrounds as regards their fathers' education – 19%
illiterate, 53% middle level (primary to 2 years at secondary), and 28% with the "bac" or above (half of whom had
studied at university). If we compare this level of the fathers'
education first with that of the corresponding group in the
WMA, and then with that of all the sample of students
questioned in 1988[5], it appears that the proportion of
WMA students' fathers who received higher education is
slightly higher than that found in the other categories of
students (11% and 22% respectively of fathers with diplomas)[6].

– Roughly one-quarter of the WMA students came
from families with members in the military (father or
brother). This percentage is slightly lower than that found
for the men officers (one-third).

– All or almost all the students had been obliged to do
military training when they went to secondary school. They
had therefore already become familiar with wearing a uniform. The same applies, moreover, to the men.

– 25% of the female military students were preparing or
hoped to prepare a university diploma, during or after their
training at the WMA[7]. A small number (about ten) wanted to
specialise, after obtaining the diploma, at one of the higher
military institutes.

As for the sample of student officers interviewed, its
features are in line with these basic data:

– Of the 16 students questioned, all were aged between 17
and 25. 6 came from Tripoli, 2 from Missourata, 3 from Benghazi
and the surrounding area, 1 from Beida, 1 from Zliten, 2 from
Sebha and 1 from a village close to the Tunisian border.

– With one exception, they all came from families with
more than 5 children.

– The fathers' professions, like their educational levels,
varied a great deal; 5 military (2 soldiers, 1 quartermaster and 2
officers), 1 nurse, 2 primary school teachers, 4 office-workers
(administration, bank, commerce), 2 factory workers, 1 fish-
erman, 1 farmer (former nomad who had settled down).

5 See Part III of the book.
6 This is contrary to what is of course claimed "in town".
7 This is in accordance with the recommendations of Colonel Ghadafi.

– The majority of the mothers were illiterate. Only one worked outside the home (director of a craft workshop).

As well as personal/family history, the framework of the individual interviews touched initially on the following subjects[8]:

Choices and motivations

It is easy to recognise, among the *motivations* put forward by the Libyan student officers, the reasons most often quoted by other women soldiers elsewhere in the world – the liking for order and organisation, the team spirit and fellowship, sense of responsibility, or even the attraction of the uniform. The latter motivation, however, was mentioned only once in our sample, which it seems can be explained by the fact that in Libya it is possible for all women to wear the uniform as volunteers in the "People's Army".

Several other familiar motives were also encountered, such as identification with a male model (father or brother who were soldiers, grandfather who was a guard etc):

– "I wanted to be a soldier like my big brother",

– "As a child I was allowed to carry my grandfather's guard's rifle".

It is more significant that the majority of our sample explained and justified this choice of a profession by arguments or motives directly inspired by the Libyan situation. Thus, 11 of the 16 questioned gave revolutionary and ideological convictions as their main reason for entering the WMA:

– "Before the revolution, women were not allowed to take part in public life. Colonel Ghadafi opened all avenues to women. The example of the woman soldier proves that Libyan women take part in the various aspects of the life of the country".

– "If a woman has to have the same place in society as a man, she must also be able to take part in defence, and if necessary in war".

– "Libya was an oppressed country which the revolution liberated. We, the young generation, want to take part in

---

8 Later on we dealt with the following subjects (which are discussed in Chapter II):
  – The liberated woman: definitions
  – Development of men/women relationships.
  – Relationship to money, work and time.
  – Tradition/modernity.

the revolution, we are the first to benefit from it, and we have a duty to defend what we have gained".

We also found quite frequent allusions to the situation in the Middle East and, consequently, to the necessity for women to know how to defend themselves:

– "The events in the Lebanon such as Sabra and Chatila have demonstrated the necessity to defend oneself. There, all that women could do was to shout and cry".

– "When we see what is happening in Lebanon, we understand that there would have been less trouble and victims if, instead of devoting themselves solely to their families, women had learned to defend themselves".

– "It is very important for women to be able to participate in progress and in the defence of their country".

Opposition from parents

To the question, *"Did you have difficulty in making your parents accept your choice of a military career?"*, all the students from military families (father or brother) claimed to have had only encouragement:

– "As soon as the WMA was opened, I had the idea of joining, but I was still too young. First I talked to my brother (soldier) about my plan. He encouraged me: 'If you want to do that, you must do it'. The young people in the family all agreed, my father (himself a soldier) too. The old people didn't. They didn't dare express their opinion too much. But they know that Libya is changing and nothing can be done about it".

– "I wanted to show that a woman too can be a soldier. My father and brothers weren't at all against the idea of us, women, joining the army, on the contrary, we go out together in uniform, father, daughter and son. It's beautiful to see, and my mother is very proud of it".

Among those who came from non-military families, several confessed to having encountered problems (resistance from the family, criticisms from the neighbours). Sometimes they were helped in their case by former students in their neighbourhood. Only two of them stated that they had gone to enrol alone – one by in a way blackmailing her parents, the other by arguing with them and slamming the door.

Adapting to the WMA

Did the Academy come up to their expectations? Did the

young military students find what they thought at the WMA? Was it easy to adapt? What difficulties did they encounter?

The large majority of those questioned declared that they had been in no way disappointed. The Academy closely matched their expectation of it, and was even better.

– "The WMA corresponds to how I imagined it. I even found what I didn't expect to find – for example the attention we are given here as individuals, and also the very friendly atmosphere".

– "On the contrary, I thought it would be difficult, but when I came here I felt at ease straight away".

– "I came to the WMA with a group of friends from my class. I made other friends. We are roughly the same age and we are all from the same culture. In the end it was better than I had thought".

For many of them, however, separation from their family was difficult during the first six months. A few confessed to shedding more than one tear:

– "I missed my family a lot at first. During those first six months we were completely cut off from each other. I cried about it more than once".

– "Being cut off suddenly from your parents is very hard. But we were well looked after at the WMA, we saw lots of new things, especially on organised visits to modern factories, archaeological sites etc. They explained things to us which were useful for our studies in the army".

Physical tiredness and the lack of sleep (reduced to six hours per night) were quoted as being the most difficult at the beginning. Later, for some of them, the test would be being reconciled with their parents who came to visit them after six months:

– "The most difficult thing for me was meeting my mother on her first visit here. We had parted angrily, then I managed to convince her and we were reconciled. Now my father comes to get me every week in the car for the weekend. We all get on very well again".

Day-to-day life, organisation, relationships
One of the interviewees described the day's programme, seemingly quite full, as follows:

"We are woken up at six o'clock, by the bugle. When we

first came here we were given half an hour to get dressed, later on a quarter of an hour, and in the end, 10 minutes.

Before going to training, we drink a bowl of milk or coffee. At the drill, which lasts until 10 o'clock, obviously they check on who's there. Afterwards, we have a shower and get half an hour for breakfast. The rest of the morning is spent either in lessons and study, or again in training. At 1 o'clock we change and then have lunch.

We are free until 4 o'clock, we have a nap, look after our clothes, write letters etc. From 4 o'clock until dinner-time (8 o'clock) there are 'civil' lessons. After dinner, revision of lessons for 1 or 2 hours or more. Lights have to be switched off at midnight.

In principle, we are free every week-end and we can have our parents and friends visit us outside the lessons.

To the question: "What do you think is 'the best thing' about your time at the WMA?", the answers, in order of frequency, were as follows:
– the training in the morning,
– the friendly relations between students and staff,
– the friendly and almost family atmosphere, the unity among students,
– the philosophy lessons (where they also study the Qu'ran and the *Green Book*),
– the sports – athletics, basketball.

Although on arrival the students are grouped by dormitories (the WMA takes care not to separate friends from the same school), and the working teams are generally formed by affinity (for the other things the students are divided into groups of thirty by alphabetical order), the student officers are supposed to confide in the "chief supervisor", a former student of the Academy, for all their problems and desires other than those relating to the studies. One of these supervisors described her task as follows:
– "I am in constant contact with the students to deal with their problems of a practical nature, such as going out, money, health etc. For problems of a psychological nature, in principle a specialised psychologist has to deal with them, but in fact the girls most often confide in me. Then I have to pass on the questions and problems of all kinds to my superior (also a woman officer who looks after all the groups)".

101

The system seems perfect. In any case this is confirmed by the students:

– "If I have personal problems, and that happens of course, I confide in the woman who is responsible for my group. I tell her everything. There is also a psychologist, but we hardly ever go to see her".

– "If there is something wrong and we feel a gap, an unease, we talk about it to our supervisor. She looks after us a lot".

As for contact with the teachers, it is limited to the lesson-times and generally to the content of the studies. The system of "Popular Committees" is not introduced in military establishments[9]. But, once a month, students and teachers get together to discuss the programmes and studies.

As the teaching body is mixed, we tried to find out if the students had a preferential bias towards women or men teachers.

The majority stated it did not make any difference. However, they showed a slight preference for women teachers: "They understand us better, they are closer to us". "Sometimes we talk after the lesson about other subjects such as revolutionary commitment or equality between men and women, or pedagogy. Exchanging opinions is necessary and enriching". One of the students, who had worked as a primary school teacher before going to the WMA, gave us a more concrete and precise point of view on this subject: "At school they talk to you about responsibility, independence, solidarity etc. Here, instead of talking about them, they apply these principles and teach you to apply them. Of course I like teaching, especially the very little ones. On the other hand, being a student myself here has helped me to realise faults and mistakes that I was making as a teacher. The supervisors at the WMA look after each of us well, they respect our personality, so in my turn I've learned to look after each of my pupils more". (Bernia still practices her profession of primary school teacher part-time).

---

9 On the other hand, several student officers from Tripoli said they took part in the "Basic Congresses" of the neighbourhood where they came from, as resident members.

Punishments and rewards

What is the disciplinary regime? Are punishments and sanctions applied?

According to all the interviewees, the discipline is stricter than at secondary school, but still not too hard to bear, because, they say, "the atmosphere is good" and it is "necessary to be disciplined as a soldier".

One of them tackled the problem in greater detail:

– "Even if we make mistakes, the punishments are not very hard. They are based on understanding and discussion. There are several kinds of punishment:

• for disobedience or negligence, we are made to do an extra hour of exercise while the others rest;

• for bad school work we are stopped from going out at the week-end;

• for an act of indiscipline, we are punished more severely. That can be as much as three or four days shut up (in the prison which is on site);

• finally, if nothing works, the student is expelled from the Academy (which happened this year to one girl who could not stand discipline at all).

In fact, disobedience among us is rare. The girls are aware that they have a great opportunity by being accepted into the Academy, being able to study there and then make a career. Punishment is sometimes inflicted as a test, for a reason which is a little unfair, following a minor fault, the student is sometimes kept in at the week-end. The aim there is to see what the girls are ready to accept, how far they are motivated, and if they have the will to go on to the end.

There are also collective punishments, to encourage team spirit. When a group hasn't finished the task set on it in time, or when a girl in a group has made a mistake, sometimes all the group is punished and, for example, it has to do an hour of running when the others are resting. That's the hardest thing!

At other times, we are only punished mentally, the culprit has to explain why she did this or that in front of the others, and we talk about it. Generally, we are given the opportunity to explain ourselves as to why and how we committed this or that offence.

But there are also rewards. There are even more of these than there are punishments. So, I had the right to a private

103

room three times because I was first in the end-of-term exam. I even got a watch as a present from the management, because I had been put third in the whole Academy. On that occasion the staff had organised a little party. At the end of the year the diplomas are given out with rewards for the ten best students of the year (they get videos, sports equipment etc).

Even so I have been punished sometimes, because I hadn't always done my exercises, or my uniform wasn't impeccable. In any case, there isn't any corporal punishment here. By the teaching, they avoid students committing mistakes which could merit such sanctions. At the very most, sometimes if the additional work isn't done well, you are given a slap or a kick. But then it isn't really a punishment".

Opinions on co-education

We thought it interesting to find out the opinion of our interviewees on the subject of co-education. Is identical education for children of both sexes regarded as a desexualisation factor? In their opinion, do equality and co-education have to go together? In the extreme, couldn't the WMA be merged with the MMA?

The opinions collected were as follows:

– For *the nursery and primary school*, all agreed that it was a good thing for girls and boys to be together in class. Indeed all the primary schools in Libya have already been mixed for several years[10].

– Co-education is also the norm for *Libyan universities*, and for this level our survey also revealed an almost unanimous opinion:

• "At University you get used to being together, so that later you can work together. You learn to get to know each other better".

• "Mixed education can change the image of a woman, even the one she has of herself".

– In the *secondary schools*, on the other hand, there are only a few mixed schools (only in Tripoli and Benghazi). On the subject of co-education at this educational level, which coincides with the stage of puberty, opinions varied a great deal.

10 In this respect Libya is only just behind France, where co-education only became the norm in 1972.

Some argued for the development of co-education as the basis for egalitarian, friendly and collegial relationships. This opinion was summarised as follows by one of them, a former secondary school teacher who had become a soldier:

● "Co-education, even at puberty, is a good thing. Young people get used to seeing themselves as equals. If they are separated, they will unconsciously think that they are different. We find that children educated together behave more normally towards each other. Boys from non-mixed schools first look at the girl's body, and only then at the rest".

Others, on the other hand, argued for separation of the sexes during this time of life when everybody is looking for their identity:

● "At the age of puberty, it is better to separate girls and boys, as biologically they are too different. Later, they can be put together again".

● "For the secondary school, it is better to separate them, as at that age their personality has not yet stabilised".

● It's mainly a question of programme. Boys are less mature, in general they understand less quickly at that age. Also, they don't have the same centres of interest".

As for the situation of the WMA, a certain consensus came out to acknowledge that since it was a new institution and still not accepted very well by the public at large, co-education was to be avoided:

● "The WMA is a boarding establishment. If girls live there, and there were boys too, they could get ideas, they could be disturbed, or even seduced, indeed be wrongly accused".

● "The WMA is a new experiment in our society. Now already, so many things are said about this establishment, so we mustn't add to them".

Some student officers thought that the Military Academy would become a mixed institution in future. Already, some noted, some of the lessons and exercises were taking place together. Furthermore,

● "In any case, in war we have to fight together".

Another expressed as follows the problem that she saw with the WMA being single-sexed:

● "Although for the exercises we are more at ease with each other, too much intimacy among women is not recommended either".

Finally we will mention this "feminist"-inspired opinion, motivated by the pilot nature of the establishment:

– "The WMA is a unique institution. Its reputation is talked about everywhere. It it were mixed, this result would be attributed to the presence of men. Today, at any rate, its success is definitely due to women!"

Contact with the university

A quarter of the student officers follow studies at university in parallel to the WMA programme (by being let off some lessons at the Academy). We questioned those concerned on what, in their opinion, could be a difference between them and the "civil students".

The replies were very significant:

– "We are the best". "We were selected at the beginning, and military discipline is the strongest". "We have been trained to apply what we were taught".

Justified or not, this attitude is characteristic; the student officers have a high opinion of themselves and, as we saw, there is a very strong emotional investment within their own group. We can conclude, in short, that their identification with the image and model of the woman officer as presented by the official discourse is quite complete. This is again confirmed by the information obtained about their career plans.

Future plans

All the student officers in the sample studied said they intended to follow a military career, either after completing studies started at university, or by preparing to enter one of the higher specialisation institutes, or again by direct assignment into the army when they left the WMA. But also, with the exception of two of them, all wanted to get married later and set up a home:

– "It's natural, it's biological, but I wouldn't like to have as many children as my mother, as I also want to carry on working".

– "I will get married later, preferably to a military colleague".

Two girls, on the other hand, rejected the prospect of marriage. They argued as follows:

– "Society needs women officers a lot more than it needs mothers. I want to dedicate myself totally to my profession".

– "I have taken a vow of celibacy as a revolutionary nun. I intend, as a soldier, to devote myself entirely to the revolution".

What does the army represent for them?

All, without exception, talked about the "army of the people", that they wanted to serve as officers. On this subject, and although we have mentioned it before, it is not superfluous to return to this specific concept.

Foreign observers have often spoken, on the subject of the Libyan regime, of the open competition, even opposition, which characterised the duality between the classic army and the "army of the people", at least at the time when the two institutions co-existed (that is until Summer 1988). There is no doubt that disputes and ideological conflicts, even physical confrontations, acts of violence or insubordination expressed the profound distrust and even the hostility of the professional army towards the "rising of the masses"[11]. It is quite clear, furthermore, that the difficulty, if not the impossibility, of assessing the extent of this phenomenon is real and lasting.

It is a fact that in the eyes of the student officers, men and women, there has been a merger of the two bodies, and integration of the classic army into the army of the people[12]. This, at any rate, is how the WMA students, like those of the MMA, and their superiors, presented the situation.

As an illustration we will give here two passages from interviews, one given by the director of an MMA, an old realistic soldier, and the other by a student at the WMA, more idealistic. Both, in their own way, perfectly summarise this point of view.

For the colonel-director "talking about the disappearance of the army, as Ghadafi does, means that from now on each citizen provides his share in safeguarding peace in this country. A necessity for a small population, and, what is

11 Cf. Chapter II of Part I.

12 This obviously does not exclude the muted and persistent hostility from certain elements.

more, a strategic necessity because of the ideas and options which came out of the revolution. In the Jamahirya, we are living under a constant threat. It is better for the whole population to be trained and for the whole population to take part in setting up the defence. For us, the professional military, we will keep our rank in the army of the people, as we have become its professional specialists. The people's army will not stop needing high-level technicians, you only have to think of all the new armaments which are being invented and which can be used in the world of today".

As for the student officer, whom we questioned about her possible fear of seeing the professional army disappear in future (which was to happen three years later, at least on the theoretical level), she said, without beating about the bush: "But that is precisely the aim! The army must disappear, the only army will be the people. We want to eliminate a certain idea of the army. Our target is not to have a rank, but to progressively train the people and gradually strengthen unification. The aim is not to obtain power over others, that was the case in the past for the foreign and Fascist armies. Now, in Libya, everybody is the army. And we, the professionals, are the instructors.

If we hadn't been able to develop the people in arms, there wouldn't have been women soldiers in Libya. The woman soldier is a victory of the armed people. In other countries, such as France, women don't have the same position in the army as us, even if they have the same rank. In France, a woman colonel is the result of a technical career in the army. Here it will be the result of a struggle for the power of the people. Since we want the people to govern themselves, there is a necessity for them to also be the army".

Through this statement of faith, and it was the opinion of the vast majority of the student officers at the WMA, it seems that becoming a soldier constitutes more an act of militancy than purely and simply joining a professional environment which had begun to open to them. What they express above all is that their participation in the army and the defence of the country represents, beyond the fulfilment of their personality, a personal contribution to the revolutionary project and the future of the country.

Chapter II

The WMA as an institution for the promotion of women

The WMA was created not only to offer women new careers as soldiers and to train a few hundred more officers each year. It was primarily and above all intended to become one of the instruments for changing mentalities.

The aim of this academy, beyond professional military training, was thus the promotion of women in the widest sense. According to this theory, the female Libyan soldier, incarnating the image of the liberated woman, would be a mechanism for change – and not the least important – at the heart of the Libyan revolution as imagined by Colonel Ghadafi and his team.

How does this instrument of social transformation actually work? How do the student officers see their role of provocative innovators? What personal interpretation do they give to this theoretical role in the psycho-social reality? And to start with, what does a "liberated woman" represent for them?

1. DEFINITION OF A LIBERATED WOMAN

The definitions that they gave individually at their interviews revealed the way in which they saw the "liberated woman". The characteristics quoted most often were:

Sense of responsibility

This was mentioned by several women officers, who stressed that they knew the limits – physical, moral and religious – of the liberties that they were demanding:

– "It's a woman who knows how to use her freedom in a healthy and proper way".

– " . . . A woman who isn't supervised, but who herself knows her responsibilities and doesn't abuse her liberty".

– "A woman who is liberated to a certain extent and who doesn't go further in her relationships with men".

– "A woman who can be trusted".

Emancipation from prejudices

– "It's a woman who has freed herself from all prejudices".

– "It's a woman who has escaped from the bonds of tradition".

– "A woman freed from slavery".

Equality with men

– "A liberated woman can do the same things as a man, within the limits of her physical strength".

– "She takes part in all areas – military, political, and social".

– "She doesn't feel inferior to men, and has confidence in herself".

– "It's a woman who works, who does the same work as a man, and who also works at home, at the same time being able, like men, to take part in the defence of her country".

Spirit of openness

– "It's a woman who knows what's happening in the world, who follows the news".

– "A cultivated woman who has gone beyond elementary things and prejudices".

– "A woman who isn't closed in on herself, who accepts science and new things".

To sum up, the liberated woman as perceived by the student officers was someone who had gone beyond the guardianship of men, who was open to progress and development, who was responsible, and who demanded to be treated as an adult, even as an equal, within the limits of her physical strength[1].

To the question: *"Do you think you yourselves are 'liberated women'?"*, the responses were on the whole positive. But some thought they had still not yet quite reached the critical stage:

– "I feel I'm on the way there".

– "Yes, I am more or less".

– "I will really be liberated when I can persuade other men and women of my ideas, when I succeed in communicating my conviction of the equality of men and women. I feel it is as a duty and I really want to do that".

How had they become "liberated women?" Two main factors seem to have played a role; firstly, the open minds of the parents and more broadly speaking the family environment, sometimes thought to be more liberal or more democratic than average, and secondly the direct influence of the official discourse:

– "The fact that I am a liberated woman is thanks to my parents who gave me permission to come to the WMA, and also thanks to Moammar (Ghadafi) who is leading our revolution".

– "I became one thanks to the revolution, and my parents, who in the end allowed me to come to the WMA" (after an initial refusal).

– "I became a liberated woman thanks to my family, who have modern ideas. I was already a bit liberated when I came to the WMA, as my parents didn't force me to think like them".

– "I'm a liberated woman today because of myself, my parents, who are more democratic than others, but also because of the revolution and society".

---

1 See the interview with Khairia, a woman officer pilot in the Air Force, in Appendix B.

– "I'm liberated because of the revolution and the Leader's thinking, also thanks to my parents, who encouraged me, and my friends, who set me an example".

We thus found that, according to those taking part, the official discourse helped to make them aware of a change which was necessary and possible. It provoked in these young women aspirations to new roles and a new status for women in general. By analysing the responses noted on fundamental subjects of everyday life; families and children, work, money and time, we are now going to see how these new representations and convictions cause a modification in attitudes and behaviour. We will then verify that the results of the survey faithfully reflect the Leader's ideological vision. We will also see that the change in attitudes and behaviour is shared quite widely, particularly among the male soldiers of the staff at the WMA, those men who with the women student officers represent the "new élite", the formation of which was precisely what Colonel Ghadafi wanted.

2. DEVELOPMENT OF RELATIONSHIPS BETWEEN MEN AND WOMEN; THE FAMILY

Since the institution of the family is regarded as the basis of Jamahiryan Society, it is not surprising that marriage is its corner-stone. In this respect we are therefore obliged to make a distinction between the quantitative and qualitative aspects.

Whatever the necessities of a policy which supports a rising birth rate – Libya is a country which is largely under-populated – today the legal age for marriage for both partners is fixed at 20. This ruling by the authorities seems to reveal both the legislator's concern for equality (the same nubility for both sexes), and a desire to enhance the value of the social institution of marriage (by extending the gap between puberty and nubility, formerly non-existent), and thus a desire to protect the individual – the woman in particular.

In the official declarations, qualitative improvement of the family is presented as an essential requirement: "Families are not happy", says Ghadafi, "because they are based on domination and injustice". He goes so far as to define the institution of the family in Arab countries as a real fool's deal for women, comparing the practices from before the "Camp David Agreements" (sic), that is what, from his point of view, can pass for the standard contract between a winner and a loser. Nevertheless, social relationships, loyalty, the respect due to one's father and mother, one's husband and brothers, are and remain sacred. So Ghadafi takes care to add: "These values are only rejected when the family stops you from realising your legitimate aims".

It is revealing that in our sample only one of the interviewees went to this extreme, admitting that she enroled at the WMA against her family's wish. Attachment to the family, to the parents – both parents – seems to have remained very strong for all the other girls (but nonetheless it had in no way disappeared completely for the one who had broken off from her family. She pointed out that she had quickly been reconciled with her parents). The results of the survey show that in the eyes of the student officers it was less the relationship to the other generations that was changing and transforming than the relationship within the same generation. This opinion was reflected both by the 20 interviews[2] conducted with the female officers, and also by the discussions held with the male soldiers on the staff at the MMA (women's responses will be marked (W) and men's (M).

Although the woman's duty to respect the man was upheld (but it had been transformed into a mutual obligation), woman's obedience and subservience to man were rejected outright. The argument was as follows – men and women now had the same level of education, their judgements were of equal value, and from the moment that they were equal there was no reason to ask a woman to be under the power of her husband, her brother, or her paternal uncle, just because they were men. The statements on this point all went in the same direction:

– "Blind obedience to one's husband or brother must no longer exist since men and women became equal. We have the same education. Men can be wrong in their judgements just as much as we can".

2 i.e. 16 student officers, plus 4 female officers from the staff.

– "Before, husbands had all the rights, they hit women for nothing. Now we have become equal human beings. Nobody has the right to exercise his strength against the other. We have to talk together and try to understand each other".

According to both our male and female interviewees, the duty to obey and be subservient had therefore been eradicated by education and up-bringing, which allowed a new relationship based on dialogue and understanding. In this spirit, it was logical that the institution of marriage had to be adapted, as a priority. However, on the subject of the "traditional" marriage arranged by parents and often between "cousins", the women's opinions varied. Although none of the interviewees would consent to marrying against their own wish, and although all stressed the importance of understanding and mutual agreement in marriage, these young women would be prepared to accept their cousin for a husband if he showed himself to be more inclined to understand them and appeared in fact closer to them. For the same reasons, but negatively, marriage to a foreign husband (or wife) would be discouraged because they would be too far apart culturally. As for the concept of marriage as a strategic alliance between lineages, a system dear to the patriarchate, it was on the whole rejected; none of the women questioned would agree to sacrifice themselves to this aim. They would continue to contract marriage within the agnatic group, but the choice of husband would no longer be a parental prerogative.

As for polygamy[3], it was totally rejected as an "injustice against women". Ghadafi, for his part, condemned it outright as an institution "contrary to the Qu'ran", which, he pointed out, only allowed it in one single case – to protect widows and orphans (of which there were doubtless many in the Prophet's time). He was furthermore to add, in a very ideological vision, the argument of equality: "If we allow polygamy for one side, the other side will be entitled to demand polyandry". Our interviewees themselves did not

3 Polygamy has never been widespread in Libya. The 1973 census showed that 96.7% of the families were "monogamous", 3.2% polygamous with 2 wives, and 0.1% with more than 2 wives.

refer to religion. But they did not forget the non-equalitarian aspect:

– "Polygamy is a great injustice for women. It isn't possible for a man to be fair to two wives at the same time".

– "It's very unfair to make the first wife share her husband with another".

Although the notion of the couple claimed to be based on understanding between two people, and mutual trust had to be established instead of and in place of repression, the couple had not become autonomous in the Jamahiryan conceptual system. On the contrary, the couple would continue to be an integral part of the family and the tribe. It is true that it was no longer formed by a transaction between men, it joined together all the members concerned, men and women. But if the latter could now refuse any suitor, there was no question of them choosing their future partner without obtaining their parents' consent:

– "If my fiancé didn't get on with my family, it would be hell for all of us, for me with his family, and for him even more so".

– "It's better to be from the same social background; my parents must like and accept my future husband. This way you integrate better into the two families".

Despite this (sizeable) concession to collectivity, the inter-personal relationship within the couple was therefore inspired more by the model of friendship than that of love-passion; the sexual relationship thus became an ingredient of the relationship as friends. More delicate, uncertain, and ambiguous was the problem of relationships between the two sexes outside the framework of marriage.

According to the responses received, friendship between men and women could exist; it even existed already but still remained rare:

– "Yes, I believe in friendship. My sister, moreover, has a real male friend, but they have no intention at all of getting married, there's nothing more between them".

– "Yes, I have male friends, and I prefer them to female friends. It's a more relaxed sort of friendship and more sincere".

– "No, I haven't got any male friends. You can only have a relationship as a friend with a man within marriage".

So, for our interviewees, although the taboo of the veil[4] and not talking to men had disappeared, the one of sexual relationships outside marriage was still firmly in place. The responses of the most "emancipated" revealed this:

– "It has become normal for me to see men and go out. But I don't go any further in my relationships with men. Being liberated isn't the same thing here as in America or Europe. We keep the habits and customs of the country. We are liberated women in our own way and in our own time".

The definition of women's liberation given by the interviewees confirmed this idea; a liberated woman was one "who knows her limits and who doesn't abuse the trust placed in her". Here, and here only, had the real change taken place – the "new woman" now relied on herself, not on the protection or the supervision of another (or others); she felt capable of defending herself. On this point, it is appropriate to quote a provocative passage from a Ghadafi speech, made in 1982, before a group of students' parents: "Some say: Watch them! Why should we watch them? They aren't hens! Let them watch themselves! And also, they are armed, they only have to shoot at anyone who goes beyond the limits! It's better to defend oneself than to be watched, talking about watching them is to humiliate them".

On this subject it is interesting to note that the young women officers referred not to the *Green Book*, but to customs and traditions. Although religion was not mentioned here, we should perhaps point out that the Qu'ran recommends purity of the body and being true to one's feelings, but it is particularly restrictive with regard to adolescent sexuality (although it is referring there to both sexes). In the Jamahirya – theory and reality – the woman's body is not "liberated" in the same way as it is nowadays in the West or elsewhere (cf. USSR, China etc). It should also be stressed that abortion is strictly forbidden. The same also applies to prostitution.

Although relationships between young people of the same generation were characterised by progressive development, this statement cannot be generalised, as the relations of

4 See Part III, Chapter III.

this generation to their elders were not undergoing equivalent changes:

– "Obedience of the husband doesn't exist any more, but for the father it's different; he is of the other generation, he has acquired experience and wisdom".

– "You must always ask older people's advice".

– "Family relationships don't change when children are educated. We respect our parents just as much, even if they are illiterate. And we aren't ashamed of them, like in Europe" (a male officer who had spent some time in Scotland).

Didn't the generation conflict exist in Libya? To the question: "In what respect are you different from your mother and your grandmother?" the responses clearly showed a certain difference of behaviour, but in reality, we found a deep similarity below the apparent opposition:

– "Yes, I'm different to my mother and my grandmother, it's the difference between generations. Everything has changed. All my generation, or almost, live differently to the old one".

– "There's a big difference between generations. My mother spent her youth in ignorance; she didn't have the opportunity to be educated, she didn't go out".

– "No, there isn't a big difference between my mother and me. My mother has given me an idea of what women were like before, I explain to her what it is to be a daughter of the revolution. We complement each other".

– "The difference between us isn't great, there are only minor points. Since my mother did military training we have become even closer".

– "My mother and grandmother have the same opinions as me. The only difference is that they didn't have the opportunity to put their ideas and convictions into practice".

These different responses can, it seems, be summarised as follows; the mother-daughter relationships reflected all the difference of the situations between two generations in the same society going through total change, but in many respects the ideas and aspirations within the two generations of women corresponded, it could be said that the frustrations of the mothers nourished the ambitions of the daughters.

The fact that a rather extensive complicity with the mother was thus revealed must in no way obscure the fact that the daughter's relationship with her father would be more orientated towards conflict. It is true that the latter as the father remained surrounded by deference and respect, but he no longer incarnated undisputed and infallible authority:

– "He now has to respect his daughters in their personalities, and give them the same liberties as his sons".

It is interesting to compare these opinions with a declaration of Ghadafi himself: "Today, each of you sees yourself dominated by your parents whereas they can't dominate your brother. Why? Because one is of the female sex and the other of the male sex, and it's a blatant injustice. If there has to be domination, then let parents exercise it over all the children; and if there is liberty, let everybody benefit from it! Why should there be this segregation? Because this one, God made it female, so it must be humiliated, whereas that one, that He wanted to be male, can claim liberty. Girls must rebel and free themselves" (1982).

From the moment that the parents did not respect this rule of conduct, could the daughter assume the right – which could even become a duty – to oppose the paternal will? Would she be prepared to go as far as breaking off from her father? The right to refuse was clearly expressed not only by the student officers, but also in the sample of young people to whom we submitted a judgment test; we will come back to this later.

In the same way, the problem of relating to men from the older generation was encountered within the army. In this context, women found themselves not only in a situation of strict equality with men, but now even sometimes in a superior position in the hierarchy. According to the interviewees of both sexes, this situation did not present major problems within the same generation. On the other hand, this would not be entirely true for older people:

– (M) "Yes, it's a bit difficult at the beginning for masculine pride to accept orders from a woman. But in any case, I respect her as a soldier, and outside the army I see her as a woman".

– (W) "Yes, I can quite easily imagine having men under my command. Why not? It's a question of technical competence".

– (W) "Yes, I have men under my command. It isn't difficult to command men of our generation. With the older one, it's different; they aren't yet used to these new relations with women".

– (M) "Middle-aged soldiers often complain. They think it isn't possible for them to agree to serve under orders from a young girl".

3. RELATION TO MONEY, WORK AND TIME

The "dowry"[5] and the "mahr"[6] in Libya as in any Arab-Moslem society, are among the important traditional institutions, but here their amounts are among the highest. It is true that in other countries the institution has begun to lose its importance with the education of women, as their professional diplomas give them new options for protecting their futures. In Libya, on the other hand, it seems that this is not the case, and that "university" women demand – in a sense which is indeed bourgeois – as much as if not more than their less educated sisters. It is true that Libyans of today place great value on "diplomas" (more than on professional training as such) and that such a consideration has been able to have its influence. The fact remains that, in a system claiming to have its roots in socialism, the social "utility" of the traditional institution is no longer evident at all and we could have expected, from a system claiming to be especially egalitarian, real attacks on the dowry. Economic reasons also combine with the ideological motives; the import of gold (from Turkey in particular) has always constituted a certain drain on currency, and the phenomenon was made more noticeable during the crisis following the second oil shock.

Colonel Ghadafi has on several occasions openly criticised this institution of the dowry and the hoarding that it involves. But, like the other traditions, he has never really attacked it directly. The statements of the young women officers echoed his attitude. For them, the dowry was a

5 The dowry paid by the man to his future wife consists of two parts, one of which goes to the couple for their home, while the other becomes the woman's personal property. For her, it constitutes a guarantee that she will not remain without resources if her marriage were to end.

6 The mahr represents the gift made by the fiancé to his future wife's parents.

somewhat out-of-date institution, and, in their opinion, it would disappear "by a natural death" with the change in mentalities:

– "A very large dowry is a mistake, women aren't walking gold exhibitions".

– "Money is something which comes and goes, the 'material' aspect is not really important in the relationship between two people. It is feelings and understanding which matter most".

Although sterile accumulation of material property was criticised, saving and investment were not. Ghadafi himself publicly encouraged people to open bank accounts, and this direction seemed to be followed quite a lot by the young. In our sample of students, bank accounts were still quite rare; this is easily explained by the modest incomes at their level, but also by the close links maintained with their families and their fathers in particular. So sometimes the father could open a bank account for his daughter, unless he himself provided what she might need (a car, for example). But the responses of the members of staff at the WMA, men and women together, show that women were turning more and more frequently to a modern personal management system:

– "Before, I used to put my money in a drawer at home, but since the Leader's speech two years ago I pay it into a bank account".

– "There are quite a few women who have bank accounts, almost as many as men".

Furthermore, the official encouragement to use the institution of the banks is not necessarily contradictory to the desire to one day see the use of money disappear. For Ghadafi it remains a sign and a symbol of inequality in society. The *Green Book* says of income (the range of which is very narrow in Libya) that the individual can use it as he wishes, except for exploiting other people, but he relativises the role of money a great deal by emphasising other values. The interviews at the WMA reflected this:

– "I'm not attached to money or material questions".

– "We don't work for money, we work for the interest of the profession, for our own future, and for the country".

– "We didn't come here for the money".

The majority of the girls did not seem to aim for control of their income as a priority; after taking what they needed for day-to-day living (roughly half of what they earned), they often put the rest into the hands of the family collective, generally managed by the father, of if he were absent, by the mother, and more exceptionally by both parents. What is more, they showed themselves to be largely inclined to leave the decisions regarding the use of their savings to this same family collective:

– "In accordance with the theory (of the *Green Book*) and our customs, we share".

As for men, they did not demonstrate the same attitude towards money. Doubtless closer to social realities, they saved with a number of precise goals, in particular to save up the dowry:

– "Before marriage, men have a greater responsibility than women, buying the house, jewellery etc. After marriage it isn't the same thing. They (the couple) share the responsibilities".

But let us return for a moment to the women's idea of money, to the role and the power that they attribute to it. Although our interviewees said money was not something which was essential, several comments are to be made on this subject. According to Islam, a man has to provide for the household budget, and the wife is entitled to dispose freely of her own income. Furthermore, young women officers, even from modest backgrounds, were not really obliged to help their family economically (in this country the notion of real poverty has become hazy in one generation). Age and ideology helping, we can understand that, as young officers, they were little concerned with the material sides of everyday life. On the other hand, a few interviews conducted with men of their age and background give us a glimpse of a potential source of misunderstanding and conflict in this respect. Although the latter agreed to the principle of their future wives working professionally, they seemed in no way to neglect the economic element, declaring that they hoped for a financial contribution to the household from their future wives, while at the same time emphasising the importance of personal fulfilment and joint participation in social and political life:

– "I prefer a wife who works, as she is regarded as educated, therefore capable of bringing up her children. And then, she will earn money" (M).

– "A woman who works continues to progress, she is still learning every day, she stays in the swing of things. And also she will contribute financially to the household" (M).

Here it is significant that, contrary to what was found elsewhere (particularly in Algeria and Morocco), the Libyans questioned showed no reticence or complex at all about accepting the possibility of a financial contribution to the family budget from the wife. So a novel kind of behaviour was outlined which was clearly demonstrated by the following statement:

– "It's normal to fulfil the material needs of the household together, there is no shame in the husband no longer bearing all the responsibility alone".

Other answers from officers interviewed show that for them a good wife and mother was one who was both qualified and personally fulfilled, she no longer needed to keep herself constantly at her husband's and her family's disposal, this means it was accepted that she worked, that the jobs at home were to be shared amongst everyone.

Did the women soldiers see their future in this way? How did they imagine they would organise their future lives? And what would be the place of the child in this new-style family? It seemed to emerge from the interviews with the women soldiers that they effectively credited the men of their generation and their environment with a capacity for change which was equal to or greater than what they themselves aspired to:

– "A lot of them now help at home. In our generation, it's normal to share the tasks, we are equals".

– "Our soldier colleagues are not at all like the men of our fathers' generation. They are real allies for us".

Although the definition of the "liberated woman" given by the interviewees rarely mentioned work as a factor in liberation, all, or almost all, stated that they wished to continue their profession when they were married and had become mothers. Moreover, they seemed to find it quite natural that their future husbands would accept this activity outside the home:

– "I will never marry a man who would want to stop me from exercising my profession".

How, therefore, did they think they would be able to combine their two future functions, that of mother and that of soldier? The main point was that they referred to managing time. Firstly, they declared, you had to organise your daily life in a strict fashion (and as soldiers they thought they would be better prepared than other women to do this), then, they thought it necessary to restrict the size of the family ("otherwise we will become slaves"). All those who envisaged getting married, that is 90% of them, wanted "to have only three or four children, not six or seven as still often happens in Libya today". But in particular, they insisted, it would be essential for all the members of the family, husband and children, girls and boys, to share the various tasks and chores at home. Finally, in a reasonable and aware manner, they thought that "to really have a career" was hardly compatible with a normal family life, and that was the sacrifice that had to be made if they wanted children.

So the modern concepts which generate choice (the size of the family, the family budget, the place and role of the child) were beginning to be integrated into a general life plan. Motherhood was no longer "the inevitable", they would decide the number of children and the time they were born[7]. In short, motherhood, like fatherhood, would be regarded as personal fulfilment. Although procreation, the arrival of the child, into this rich and socialist, therefore egalitarist and protective, Libya no longer represents economic and social security as before, they no less continue to play one of the most important roles on the collective and national level. Having children remains a priority, as the Jamahirya is a country with insufficient population, largely dependent on immigration at all levels, immigration which is expensive and conflictual[8]. Our interviewees on the whole showed that they were aware of this:

– "Our duty as women is to educate ourselves, then to

7 This is reflected in the statistics, which show a high birth rate at the beginning of the summer, particularly for women teachers.

8 Foreigners in Libya at any given time represent almost 30% of the population (from the Far East, the Philippines, South Korea, Eastern Ethiopia, and in particular the neighbouring countries, Egypt, Morocco, Tunisia and Sudan).

123

have four or five children, in turn to bring them up and educate them, so that one day we and they will be able to replace the foreigners".

– "It isn't just for myself that I want to have children, it's also for our country and for its future".

Was this a rejection or a reinterpretation of the old values? The overall attitude of our sample to the traditions consisted rather of subjecting them to a critical examination, in a way sorting them out:

– "A liberated woman can remain attached to certain traditions, as there are good ones and bad ones, or rather each tradition has a good and a bad side. For example, relationships between parents and children, that's positive, but family oppression is negative".

– "Each generation has its ideas and its customs. You keep what is good and reject the rest. I think that with culture and education you can drop certain traditions. The next generation will doubtless do the same after us, depending on the new knowledge and techniques".

– "There are traditions which are valid and others which are invalid. For example, staying at home isn't good for a woman, as society needs her".

On the other hand, they showed themselves generally inclined to keep the traditions which were based on "true values", in particular those which were based on religion:

– "We remain attached to religion perhaps even more than our mothers, even if we reinterpret it in a modern sense, according to the requirements of today's life".

So they thought that wearing the veil could be left to each person's judgement, as the costume (like, moreover, the uniform) was not really essential:

– "With education, people have understood that dress isn't really important. Trousers are very well accepted. There are girls who continue to wear the veil and the farashia, but they also wear the uniform. There are also some who wear the veil but who don't practise religion, and others the other way round. The latter are generally respected more in today's society".

So we have just seen how the transition from tradition to a certain modernity is taking place under the auspices of the WMA, the "nursery" of the liberated Libyan woman. But what is the real influence of these student officers and these women officers as a "new elite"? Has the "model" which they represent been echoed either within their immediate environment or elsewhere in the Libyan population? And how are the institution and its students judged from outside? These questions, the necessity to understand the impact in society of a creation which was certainly idealistic but no less concrete and living, led us quite naturally to expand our field of vision, and to try and confirm certain hypotheses or deductions built up in the generally quite restricted context of the Women's Military Academy.

Chapter III

The WMA as seen by others

In a society as traditionalist as Libya in the 70s, the extension of compulsory military training to girls, and then the foundation of the Women's Military Academy, constituted gestures of political importance and resolutely feminist inspiration on the part of the authorities. In fact, the application of the doctrine known as "the people in arms" to women was to provoke more controversy and opposition in the people's minds than all the rest of the programme. An army colonel, a former director of one of the military academies, spoke in these terms:

"I've been a professional soldier for more than twenty years, and I was totally in favour of women participating in the army and in defence. But it wasn't at all easy to persuade the people.

The People's Army was formed in 1977. We started training the male population straight away, followed by the women. The people weren't at all enthusiastic, there was even a lot of resistance. The army was seen as something bad in itself, like a special mission, a necessary evil. It wasn't popular. And when, what is more, we wanted to bring in women, we saw almost all the men rise up against us.

The proposal to extend compulsory military training to girls in secondary schools was discussed at length in the country's Basic Congresses. In the end it was accepted, but after what efforts! The argument which prevailed was the danger of imperialism and the necessity to defend ourselves and protect peace in this country."

The Libyan population had gradually been brought round to the image of girls wearing military uniform. Nonetheless, the opening of the WMA in 1979 was still a great shock to sensibilities. And although the establishment had already been in existence for quite a few years when we carried out our study, the WMA was still the subject of frequent passionate discussions. As we were not able to carry out a general survey among the different categories of the population, we tried to supplement what we were told by the student officers interviewed with group discussions on the same subject among the student circles[1] in Tripoli. Also, in 1987, we conducted an opinion poll on the presence of female elements in the armed forces among a representative sample of student officers from the MMA.

An analysis firstly of the opinions of the students on the criticisms heard against them or their establishment, and then of the views of the students from Tripoli University on the same subject, leads us to conclude that opinions were divided and opposed along a distinct line.

In brief, the opinions expressed show that neither the militarisation of women, nor their participation in the defence of the country were really disputed; they were largely accepted by the Libyan people. But on the other hand, the existence of the Women's Academy as an institution was criticised in that it went against the country's traditions and customs, it was in some way against nature: "In our country, a girl has to live with her parents until she gets married". "The WMA separates girls from their parents". "There is no guarantee of morality there". "I don't think it's right for her to mix with just anybody at the Academy". "We aren't against militarisation of women, but we are against immorality". "Our criticisms of the WMA are criticisms of women who don't obey traditions

1 Five groups, each of 6 students, were questioned.

any more, who don't respect the taboos, who no longer conform to the patriarchal rules and standards".

The case of Safia (the daughter of a former leader from the time of the monarchy) teaches us a great deal. After taking the "bac" (with distinction), she really wanted to go to university with the intention of becoming a civil engineer. Her parents accepted this choice, although not without some reservations and criticisms. However, before going to university, Safia had to go through a brief period of military service. But for her, going to the army, even if only for a period of 7 days, was unthinkable. Her mother's argument was: "How could we let her go there? We don't even know who she will be sharing her room with . . . " What is more, her father was away (on a trip abroad), they couldn't make the decision there and then. Her brother then declared, without any hesitation: "We (the two of them, father and son) will certainly decide that if going to university means she has to go through the army barracks, then she should give up university and stay at home". Meanwhile, Safia was no longer eating or sleeping. But it all turned out well for her, it was the army that gave in, and gave her permission to go to university to follow her studies.

It is true that such attitudes and opinions originated mainly from the "old generation" and the "bourgeois" backgrounds of the old regime. The student officers, however, acknowledged that the Academy was also criticised by quite a few close or nearby families, those of the neighbours, for example. On this subject it is interesting to note that the majority of the WMA students questioned described their own families as more liberal or more democratic than those of their fellows. Out of sixteen students interviewed, only two girls met with strong opposition at home to their choice of the Military Academy.

As for opinions among the students at Tripoli University, apart from a small number who rejected outright the concept of women as soldiers, most of them thought that the opening of the army as a career to women was a positive thing in itself. They described the foundation of the WMA as useful, indeed an important step in the process of the emancipation of Libyan women. Some, however, expressed doubts about the quality of the military instruction given there. In short, the WMA was still found difficult to accept, at least by a part of Libyan society, more in that it appeared to contradict the traditional values.

What was the opinion of the young generation's male officers on this subject? What did they think of women taking part in the armed forces?

To find out, we drew up the following questionnaire, to which 46 student officers were invited to give their answers:

"1. What are your future plans when you leave the Academy, after getting your diploma?
– Do you intend to follow a specialisation in one of the specialised military academies? Yes/No.
– After your diploma, do you want to be posted directly to an army barracks? Yes/No.
2. Would you prefer to marry a woman officer or rather a woman who was not a soldier?
    – Yes, I would prefer to marry an officer colleague.
    – No, I would prefer to marry a non-military woman.
    – It doesn't matter to me whether she is a soldier or civilian.
3. Would you prefer your wife to give up work and stay at home when married? Yes/No.
4. Do you think that a soldier wife can be as good a wife and mistress of the house as another wife? Yes/No.
5. Do you think that women have to take part in the defence of their native country in all areas of combat?
    – Yes, women must participate in everything, even in close combat.
    – Yes, women must participate in combat, but they must remain at the rear.
    – No, women must not take part in war and combat.
6. In a few words, give your opinion on women soldiers."

Analysis of the opinions expressed on women soldiers in general, broken down into three categories, shows that:
– A minority of men student officers (9%) stated that they were totally against the presence of women in the army (and, naturally, their participation in combat):
"I don't think women can be happy outside the home.

They have to stay with their children. They have no need at all to go to military schools. It's men's business".

"I'm frightened they will lose their femininity there, they will do things against their nature. Then they won't be all right".

"To take part in the army, women have to have permission from their parents, or their husbands. Personally I'm against this participation".

– One-third (32%) expressed qualified opinions, weighing up the pros and cons, emphasising the positive aspects as well as the negative, but some concealing an attitude which tended to be unfavourable. All, with one exception, were opposed to women taking part in combat, but they allowed them to be present at the rear: "It's the new 'model', but they mustn't neglect their homes, their husbands and their children. Looking after the house and the children, that's what they were created for".

"Women who join the army are forced to sacrifice everything, to devote themselves completely to their task. They can't combine that with their family life. It's only when they have left the army and finished that phase that they can start a normal life again".

"They haven't to work in the armed forces, but to know how to use arms in case they need to".

"It's good if they're brave enough to be in the army. But they have other duties and obligations, in particular they must be the guardians of customs and religious traditions in society".

"Special tasks must be reserved for women, corresponding to their nature and their physical abilities. They must retain their femininity and their dignity".

– The majority (59%), however, showed themselves to be totally in favour of women taking part in the army (and even in close combat – 43%):

"A woman soldier is a good example of a modern woman, who fulfils her duty both to her country and her family. She shares everything with the man, including the field of war".

"The students at the WMA are very clever, they are better than the others. They get ranks, they have a specialised profession".

"Women in the armed forces are free women, who possess all their rights. They work side by side with men, in war as in peacetime".

"All the women in the Jamahirya must take part in the armed forces. The defence of the country is a duty for everybody, the enemy doesn't make a distinction".

"The Jamahirya doesn't distinguish between men and women, they are responsible for the native land together. Women must be educated and be able to help in the army as elsewhere".

"Women in the army are free women, intelligent and strong. They play their part like their brothers and must be respected. Men and women have the same place".

"Before, women were deprived of their rights, they were neglected beings, who were excluded from society. Now they have the right to work, to take part in everything, they aren't confined to their homes any more. The best ones can also take part in the army".

"As early as the time of the Prophet women took part in war; it isn't really anything new. It's logical for them to take part in the profession of arms, they represent half the Libyan population".

So Libyan women soldiers, well accepted by the majority of their "comrades in arms", whether real or potential, were apparently much less so as possible partners; only 5% of the men student officers preferred to have a military colleague for a wife, whereas 43% would rather prefer to avoid such a marriage. It should be noted, however, that for half of those questioned: "A military wife or a civil wife, it's the same thing".

As for the qualities that could be attributed to a military woman in the role of wife and mother, one-third of the responses indicated that they were in doubt. For those who thought like this, a civil partner would offer more guarantees in these areas.

To the question: "Would you prefer your wife to work or to stay at home?", two-thirds of the sample opted for a wife at home. One-third, however, stated that they were in favour of a wife who exercised a profession outside, which in the Libyan context can be regarded as a high percentage.

A breakdown of the answers by age-group (18 to 23

compared with 24 and over) and by background (illiterate father compared with educated father) revealed a positive correlation between age and an attitude favourable to the presence of women in the army (61% of the young compared with 45% of the older ones). But no correlation was revealed by the comparison with the background.

With regard to the wife working outside the home, only a slight correlation could be found with the background, the students from illiterate backgrounds being slightly less favourable to the wife practising her profession than the others. As for the age of the interviewees, it does not seem to have any influence on this subject. However, to assess the answers to this last question properly, it should be borne in mind that married women are not formally encouraged to work by the official discourses, and they do not allow this to be assimilated to a form of modernism or social progress. We will return to this fundamental debate in Part III of the book.

Analysis of the qualifying adjectives used by the male student officers in respect of women soldiers is useful and illuminating. The vocabulary used leads us to identify two categories:

– on the one hand, adjectives which give value such as "open, free, educated, proud, strong, determined, aware, responsible", are contrasted with others, depreciative or indeed pejorative, which describe women of the traditional profile: "without education, ignorant, dependant, suppressed, reified, tied, confined to home, non-participatory",

– on the other hand, recourse to a panoply of "technical" words relates more directly to the military status: "military model", "punctual", "respectful of her superiors", "making herself respected", "exemplary", "intelligent in work", "real specialist".

Of these two categories of adjectives, the first obviously expressed judgements relating to the female Libyan soldier as a liberated woman. As for those in the second category, which refer to military dominance, we found that they were quoted less often than the first ones.

On the subject of women taking part in the defence of the country, it was described:

– sometimes as an innovation: "a major new thing", "a

huge thing", "very important for the development of the country and the army";

– sometimes as following logically and naturally from development: "the consequence of equality between men and women", "the fruit of the new citizenship of women", "the effect of the application of democracy".

But those who declared themselves to be against this participation in the army and the defence of the country adopted a completely different language. They expressed:

– either a protective attitude towards women, showing their preoccupations with the fate which was likely to befall them:

"An abnormal life, dangerous for her femininity, her dignity and her honour"; "Too hard for her"; "Against her nature"; "A woman can only be happy in her home";

– or an authoritarian attitude, criticising the military role that they could play:

"She mustn't take part in military action, war is not her business"; "She must have permission" (from her father or her husband); "She has more important duties"; "The army is men's business".

This survey shows that women soldiers were on the whole already well accepted. They were certainly more so as army colleagues than as women, potential wives or mothers.

However, if we compare these different attitudes to those we encounter in other countries where the female element has been introduced into the army relatively recently, it is not unreasonable to state that Libyan female officers are regarded more positively by their colleagues than those from other countries; different studies carried out in the United States and France in particular demonstrate this[2].

In carrying out the field-study, the fact that we took the precaution of insisting on the guarantee of anonymity for the answers means that we can hope we avoided the risks of sham attitudes being expressed and obtained "the truth" of the opinions. Can we conclude that the feminist speeches of the Libyan powers, combined with the psychological action

2 E. Reynaud *Les femmes et l'armée: l'exemple américain d'intégration de la femme dans l'armée*, Paris, French Institute for the Study of War.

conducted at the level of the young officers' education, both male and female, had already borne fruit? On this subject, don't we have to take account of a kind of follow-my-leader attitude, i.e. conforming behaviour which is a transitory and circumstantial adaptation, without witnessing deep conviction or real belief in the opinion expressed?[3] Nevertheless, we cannot rule out the hypothesis that the surface desire to conform influenced, even modified, the deep convictions of the men and women questioned, to produce a real change in opinion.

Although women soldiers were still regarded by a section of the Libyan population as an outside group, with whom they did not have nor wanted to have anything in common, it seemed that such negative categorisation remained the attitude of a minority in the new generation. We can then ask how this society, still so traditional, was able to adapt so quickly to the revolutionary and feminist idea of the militarisation of women. This is a debate which continues to be the subject of many discussions even in the West.

It seems that the answer, for Libya, must be sought among a batch of disparate but convergent causes; the Libyans' past, the Islamic concept of war, the regional political situation, and, last but not least, the particular nature of Libyan feminism.

FACTORS EXPLAINING ATTITUDES OF LIBYAN POPULATION GROUPS TO THE WMA:

A. *The past*

Libya was, and has remained, a fragile country with a complex. It is fragile because it is huge and very underpopulated, and 95% economically dependant on a single resource, oil. It has a complex because for a long time it was the poorest of the poor, trampled on by Italian colonisation, harshly administered, then despoiled by a monarchal system characterised by the incompetence and corruption of a very narrow élite.

---

3 Cf. Solomon E. Asch, *Effects of group pressure on the modification and distortion of judgement, 1951.* Leon Festinger: *A History of cognitive dissonance,* Evanston, III Row. Peterson 1953, and the debate provoked by these pioneer works on social influence.

The team of Free Officers popularised ideas which in their nature would appeal to men and women who were disinherited, starved of consideration, whom the monarchy had not managed to get to. Later, the slogans of the *Green Book* such as "Power, wealth and arms in the hands of the people" found fertile ground. In this way Ghadafi began to turn this mass of tribes and small groups into something resembling a nation. And the outside world, Western as well as Eastern, did the rest; believing itself threatened by the Colonel's revolutionary and adverse ideas, it helped not a little to transform what was at the beginning only a feeling of solidarity in popular support of the régime.

But the *Green Book* is addressed to all the people, not just the male half. The approved idea of the "people at arms" logically included the idea of "women at arms". Although it is true that Ghadafi has not yet managed to make the whole population accept the principle of compulsory military service for all women (not only for students), it is to be noted that the number of married women voluntarily opting to do military training (naturally in agreement with their husbands) is increasing day by day.

B. Islam

More than Christianity, it cultivates, even makes sacred, the image of war, not only in its glorious past but also in the modern revivalist expression. Whether we refer to the old religious motives of extending and defending the Moslem land or community, or to the "jihad" (the holy struggle for the defence of God's rights) as a residual duty of the community, without doubt war has fewer negative connotations in Islam than in the Christian West.

C. The political situation in the Middle East

The subject of the Palestinian question is followed very closely in Libya. Ghadafi, who baptised his coup d'état "Operation Jerusalem", fought for the cause of the Palestinians against Israel and American imperialism from the very beginning. The fact that the situation of Lebanese and Palestinian women became a reference for the student officers (cf. reasons for joining the WMA), and that for the Libyan population as a whole the fear of American imperialism served as the main alibi for accepting the formation of the "people in arms" and the militarisation of the young women, demonstrate this factor with real and still up-to-date force.

D. *The nature of Libyan feminism*

But what has been said above does not explain everything. The apparent acceptance by the soldiers themselves to share their domain, their prerogatives, and their privileges with "the weak sex" totally contradicts what we have seen in other countries[4]. In many cases the arrival of women into the army, a real intrusion into a private domain which traditionally belongs to men, has been lived as a trauma. How, then, can we explain the positive and active role played in this respect by the professional soldiers, young and not so young, in Libya, and their direct collaboration in the creation of the WMA?

We are tempted to attribute the difference to the very particular situation of Libyan feminism. It is true that, contrary to what has happened or is still happening in most other countries, and particularly in the West, where women have often been alone in their struggle for their liberties and their right to participate, in Libya they were given them "from above" (and at least for some of them thanks to the military chiefs).

There is no doubt that the official message imposed a certain feminist attitude on the army and particularly on its officers. Opportunism and conformism did the rest. In this respect it is interesting to recall the results of several studies carried out in Europe, which have shown that the attitude of the hierarchy on the subject is particularly important; in so far as it tends to be reproduced by the men inside the units, it is going in the direction of what is perceived as the new norm, although the true opinion still remains conservative.

---

4 On this subject see the study by Emmanuel Reynaud: *Les femmes et l'armée: l'exemple américain d'intégration des femmes dans l'armée*, Paris, French Institute for the Study of War, 1984.

Without taking our analysis of the factors which explain the collective Libyan attitude any further, it seems obvious that links exist between it and its environment, that is, in more general terms, between collective psychological needs and the development of political structures[5]. For example, we think that the Libyans' need for consideration is among the profound motives which have been combined to promote the new structures of the Jamahirya, as well as the system of direct democracy which it has chosen. The existence of such links shows in particular that any comparison of institutions made outside their context (for example the WMA and a Western military college) is hazardous and questionable. Such comparisons risk leading to erroneous conclusions, as the similarity of these institutions is purely formal, while the difference in their mutual histories is a determining factor on the level of the collective psychology and their specific characters. So, on the level of motivations and attitudes in general, those of the WMA students differ a great deal from those of their Western colleagues.

The Libyan students, we found, were on the whole looking for recognition not only for themselves, but also for "the others" (for all women):
– "To show what women are capable of"
– "To demonstrate our sense of responsibilities"
– "To give women confidence in themselves".

They identified not only "with women soldiers" (the professional aspect) but with all women in terms of citizenship (political and social equality). For them the military identity was therefore in no way a dispossession of the feminine identity. Moreover, this message was on the whole well deciphered by the environment, as is shown by the descriptions of women soldiers given by the WMA students.

However, soldiers or non-soldiers, some remained prisoners of the patriarchal stereotypes concerning sexual roles; they were not able to separate soldier from masculine. This interpretation of the model of the armed woman as a model of the new woman, "the liberated woman" demonstrates a confusion, a sort of cross-breeding of the two models into

---

5 A hypothesis on the causality of political and social development, which it seems has as yet been studied little or not at all.

one – that of the soldier and that of the woman. When some interviewees (soldiers and civilians) said they never wanted to marry a student from the WMA, it was because in their eyes these women incarnated the soldier, that is aggressivity and anti-femininity. However, the image that the students wanted to present was precisely that of the woman, and not the soldier. In the event, this particular situation shows the confusion of the model guiding images[6].

The "guiding image" or model of the "liberated woman" was, at least in the beginning, a formal and prescriptive model constructed deliberately and consciously to be transmitted by propaganda. As for any abstract construction, there is a gap between the theory and the practice, a gap which in the extreme can become a source of real conflict. That is what happens when the model receives different interpretations by two associated people (as in the couple). Then, the interpretation of the reference model, if the same, that one or the other may place on it is not necessarily identical. We found such a gap regarding the relationship to money; allocating each of the partners' incomes may become a source of misunderstanding in the couple. Speaking generally, for there to be understanding within the couple, agreement on the model, on the guiding image, is obviously very important.

Even though on the whole the student officers interpreted the guiding image quite faithfully, the perception of situations and social structures remained personal and differed to varying degrees from one person to another. The guiding image could be partially and selectively interpreted, even by those who claimed to incarnate it. Some aspects were emphasised and others (intentionally or not) were ignored. The model was "consumed" in the exclusive interest of themselves, going beyond the social obligations which, however, the guiding image also expressed; it then became a justification of individual ambitions. One of the female student officers, who thus showed a tendency to only retain the "personal fulfilment" aspect, stated amongst other things "A liberated woman is a woman who has escaped from the

6 P.H. Chombart de Lauwe, *L'image de la femme dans la société*, Editions Ouvrières, 1964.

bonds of slavery and she has the right to work and to do what she wants". Here a conflict was drawn between personal aspirations and guiding image.

In the area of women's emancipation in Libya, the political will anticipated the popular (= male) will. The fact that the People's General Congress (made up at that time of 95% men) refused three times to approve certain legislative proposals concerning women (in particular the law on divorce) is an example and demonstrates the gap between the prescriptive model and the socio-cultural attitude, which could provoke open conflicts[7].

Inevitably there is sometimes conflict between the guiding image presented and the real social situations. They were claiming to liberate women, they encouraged them to take part in the life of the nation, but measures taken in favour of other population groups or in the interest of the general social programme made women the first and direct victims of these same measures (the withdrawal of the "services" and private commerce, the abolition of domesticity). The transformation of all the structures was in general favourable for them, but not systematically. There was obviously material for conflict in the practical impossibility of respecting and promoting the interests of all the population groups or categories equally at the same time.

There were also conflicts due to the multiplicity of terms of reference. Among the women officers we found a reference, which if not exclusive, was at least largely dominant in all areas of their lives, to the model presented by the *Green Book*. But the *Green Book* was not their only term of reference, they also mentioned traditions, customs and religion[8]. Was it possible for these three terms of reference to co-exist peacefully, shielded from any major conflict?

It is true that human beings have a natural tendency to create a cognitive coherence, that is to avoid the multiplication of identities which contradict each other. The effort to reinterpret traditional cultural elements demonstrates this.

7 One of these conflicts, which erupted on the topic of the proposal to militarise married women, is described by J. Bearmann, *Qadhafi's Libya*, Zed Books, London 1986, p. 242.

8 It is appropriate here to remind our readers that the *Green Book* does not mention Islam.

But the extension of such an operating practice to the religious dogma is much less evident. If, however, the three terms of reference concerned continue to co-exist without real conflict for the "first adopters"[9], it is true that in the eyes of our interviewees they belong to the same model. Their integration, their harmonisation were only possible because of a wide reinterpretation of elements from the other two models – the patriarchal and the Islamic.

Considering the topical nature of the subject, we seem justified in staying on this point for a while. While at the same time stressing the need for radical changes, Ghadafi's speeches explicitly aim to link, then to integrate, new elements into a historical continuity, and thus to create a new basis of consensus. Evidence of this is the reappropriation of certain figures from the historical past (the struggle of Omar Mukhtar against the Italians), the reinterpretation of old customs (women on palanquins, see Ch. V), or the Islamic justification at the basis of the "ijtihad", (the continual effort to interpret and re-read the Qu'ran). This step confirms the rule which says that any new culture, in order to be accepted, needs to appear legitimate and provide a certain continuity. This legitimisation is ensured by the process of integrating cultural elements from the past. As for the Islamic religion, for Ghadafi it is essentially revolutionary and progressive. For him, the revolution comes from authentic Islam, but first there needs to be a revolution within Islam and by Islam, to return to the source, to the Qu'ran, as the only expression of God's word. As for the "hadith" (or the sayings of the Prophet), he believes that through the centuries they have been largely manipulated by men, and the decline is particularly noticeable as regards the status of women[10]. This fundamental, or fundamentalist stance (although Ghadafi seems to have gone further than others by totally rejecting the "hadith"), is continuing a movement to "sweep clean" which was started as early as the XIVth century by Ibn Taymia, and continued notably by the Senoussi brotherhood in the XIXth century in Libya itself

9 A term describing the first generation of people adopting an innovation.
10 A similar argument is put forward by F. Mernissi in her book, *Le Harem politique, Le Prophète et les femmes*, Albin Michel, Paris, 1987.

(Cyrenaica). Faced with the challenge of a certain modernity, Ghadafi and his team are thus getting closer to those who today debate heritage and modernity, identity and change, a debate which has in truth gone beyond the too simplistic opposition between authenticity and modernity, between "gadim" and "jadid"[11].

Beyond rejecting the "hadith", Ghadafi went even further by introducing a distinction between the Sharia (which has remained the basic law of Libyan society) and the Qu'ran, separating the temporal from the spiritual. He says that although the Sharia is based on the Qu'ran, it is only to be regarded as a human judicial work, and like any judicial code, it is open to modification, to being adapted to the needs of a society which is itself developing[12]. Declaring that his beliefs are based on an exclusive exegesis of original Islam, recognising only the Qu'ran as sacred, revering Mohammed as the last of the Prophets, Ghadafi claims to be a real fundamentalist[13], not an "integrist".

Whether the return to the Qu'ran is put forward by him both "as the target reconcilable with the necessity for socio-cultural transformations in society, and as a means of legitimising them" (according to the analysis which Djaziri makes in his thesis)[14], or again whether it must be regarded as purely "ontological" in nature, Ghadafi from then on put himself forward as a real reformer.

However, although the reinterpretation of Islam aims at making the new model coherent, it undeniably goes against traditional Islam. Apparently well accepted by the student officers, and at least by a section of the young generation (which we must not forget was brought up in this spirit) this renewed vision of Islam is in no way accepted by all the Libyan population. Who has not already heard, in the

11 Cf. the symposium held in Cairo at the end of 1984 on "Authenticity and Modernity".

12 It does seem that corporal punishments (such as the amputation of a hand for theft) have never been applied in revolutionary Libya.

13 Mohammed did not have an assistant, and as for the first caliphs, they must only be respected according to how they respected Islam. Well, they had slave-mistresses and treated women like men's shoes" (speech 8.3.1989, before Libyan women's associations).

14 M. M. Djaziri, post-graduate thesis: *Le système politique libyen 1969–84*, Lausanne university 1987.

meetings of the political committees, exclamations such as: "The *Green Book* will not stand before the Qu'ran!" Ghadafi was naturally going to find himself in deep disagreement with the majority of the Ulemas (Moslem theologians) in the country. As for the traditional layers of society, Ghadafi's reformism-adventurism could only be rejected in a population which preferred to follow more prudently "the rules"[15].

There is certainly a conflict of terms of reference, not for the followers of the movement incarnated by the choice of the new model, but indisputably for the part of the Libyan population for which any religious reform is surely more difficult to accept than the other new values. There is here, in fact, the expression of the single and same basic conviction: "Neither intermediaries nor representatives", the leitmotif of the *Green Book*, for the social aspect is here applied to religion, to the relationship between Man and God. In Ghadafi's eyes, there can in no case be a substitute for the power of decision; each human being is responsible so has to decide freely on the appropriateness of his behaviour to the divine commands. All men are and remain equal[16].

Thus the reference to primitive Islam, the closest to the teaching of the Prophet, is not made with the simple and sole desire of reproducing an old reality; it expresses the quest and the desire to create new guiding images, new models, new identities, which come rather close to Utopia and myths[17].

"Man cannot live without myth, myth is in some way at the root of his being", says R. Bastide[18]. It could be added that those who govern men need it as well. Ghadafi's

15 "Radical Islamism constitutes the only really determined current of Libyan opposition on an internal level", says F. Souchan in his article, "Ghadafi vingt ans de solitude" (*Jeune Afrique*, 6.9.89).

16 Ghadafi bases his argument for the withdrawal of the death penalty as follows: "God has said that punishment will come on the day of the last judgement". He therefore proclaims himself to be completely opposed to the theocratic system which he has criticised violently, particularly as regards the "Rushdie affair": "If somebody governed in the name of religion, it would be a catastrophe for society, this theocratic authority would put people on the point of the sword depending on its mood, or for personal reasons" (speech 8.3.89).

17 There would be a parallel to be drawn with the reference (persistent in the Ghadafian imaginary) to the bedouin society which inspires him, but which he does not try to perpetuate.

18 R. Bastide, *Le Sacré Sauvage*, Payot, 1975, p. 83.

discourse, rich in symbols and myths, has fashioned the one of the "woman at arms". Even though in Libya it has obtained a certain reality, it is nonetheless a myth, and as such goes back to the myths of ancient times (for example that of the virgin warriors). In this sense, the Libyan female soldier remains singularly different from her Western "sister"; she is expected to be something quite different from just a "woman officer", she incarnates a model, and as such represents one of the new élites in the Jamahirya.

Chapter IV

The birth of new élites

We have just seen how the woman officer represents a model of a new woman; the liberated woman. As such, she can be regarded as a new élite[1].

The Jamahirya claims to be however, and by definition, an egalitarian society, where the social distance between groups of population must be reduced as much as possible, and where the subordination of one group to another should no longer exist. In such a society, there should barely be any place for élites anymore. What, then, should we think of these new élites who have appeared during the past few years and who are the members of the Revolutionary Committees, the Female Guards, and in particular the members of the movement of the "Revolutionary Nuns" (Rahibat Thawriya)? Apart from that, where do these élites come from and what is their role? Where do they set themselves in relation to the rest of the population?

---

1 Here we mean by élite people and groups who, as a result of the power that they hold or the influence that they exercise, contribute to the historical action of a collectivity, either by the decisions that they take, or by the ideas, feelings or emotions that they express or symbolise.

Below we are going to present the three groups in question, in each case explaining the part played by women therein.

Although the Libyan revolution tended towards the establishment of an egalitarian society, this could not claim to have been achieved overnight; for this aim new values had to be introduced and old mentalities changed. Ghadafi had stressed this necessity right from the start of the revolution. So, in his speech at the Tripoli mosque in December 1971, he was already declaring: "We must direct ourselves towards releasing a spiritual and cultural revolution, a revolution which takes place inside ourselves, so that each of us can walk on the right track". He quoted the Qu'ran: "Allah does not change what is in a people before it changes what is in itself".

So it was not enough to declare the establishment of the "society of the masses" and to officially put power into the hands of the people in order for the change to take place as if by magic. It was necessary for the people to want to and be able to play the role that had to be theirs. And in 1977, this was in no way yet the case; the conscious, active commitment of the Libyan men and women left a lot to be desired. And the directors of the revolution were not unaware of this reality, as is shown by this declaration of the commander A. Jalloud in 1980: "The weak spot in the revolution is that an avant-garde which produced the revolution in 1969 is still activating it today. We would like the people to accept their responsibilities. But we realise that if the avant-garde were to disappear, it would be fatal for the revolution; first, it hasn't happened often in history that the élite itself gives the power back to the people, then the people who have received the revolution on a silver platter hesitate about making sacrifices to defend it, as deprived people would do. These contradictions are the first danger . . . "

When, on 1 September 1978, Ghadafi declared that he was officially withdrawing from power to give himself the role of Guide of the Revolution, his aim was to act better on the level of the change in mentalities, and to himself become in some way its instrument. This goal required renewed strategies, and it was precisely in this context that the need

for new élites made itself felt and that the following groups were set up in succession:
- in 1977 the Revolutionary Committees[2]
- in 1979 the "Women Officers" (with the opening of the WMA)
- in 1980, the "Female Guards"
- in 1981 the movement of the "Rahibat" or Revolutionary Nuns.

Each of these "élite bodies" would have its own method of representation which would determine the nature of the influence that it would be likely to exercise. Their styles of behaviour would differ and the social significance that would be attached to them would help – or hinder, depending on the situation – this process of influence to unwind, as we shall see later.

1. THE REVOLUTIONARY COMMITTEES (RC)[3]

The definition of the Revolutionary Committees given by the Libyan authorities[4] is as follows: "The Revolutionary Committees are an open international movement, whose aim is to establish and consolidate the Jamahirya (the State of the Masses). They constitute an instrument the purpose of which is to promote the age of the masses and the power of the people".

Subsequent declarations or documents were to explain that the *Green Book* was both their theoretical guide and their programme of action. And it would also be explained that "although the movement has a specific political aim, it is not a political party, but more a group of propagandists, missionaries and educators at the service of the production and stabilisation of the new civilisation of the masses". For "it is a revolutionary movement which is both permanent and temporary, which has to disappear (as a structure) once

2 The first RC were formed in 1976 among the students following the "Students' Revolution". Their formation was neither systematic nor co-ordinated with a political structure.

3 There are Revolutionary Committees especially for women, and "International" Revolutionary Committees for the purpose of acquainting the world outside Libya with the Jamahiryan system.

4 See *The Revolutionary Committees*, Ed. Green Book Centre (Tripoli 1987).

the Jamahirya is consolidated and the masses have become revolutionarily aware".

The movement of the Revolutionary Committees therefore had a practical aim, and its members were invested with a concrete task, which was to promote "the age of the masses" by encouraging the population to exercise power themselves. Also, according to official sources, this aim was to be expressed in practice by organising and conducting conferences and congresses, by encouraging the population to take part in large numbers and there to express their rights and their aspirations, and finally by exercising a revolutionary control over the whole of society[5].

By carrying out the functions of organisers and educators, the Revolutionary Committees would assume revolutionary leadership for the whole of the population; in this capacity they would be charged with demonstrating themselves to be exemplary in the revolutionary domain as in the moral. However, according to the official texts, although they had to incarnate "the New Man", they could not regard themselves as "élites" compared with other groups of citizens.

Anyone who wanted to belong to a Revolutionary Committee had to be aware that they would not have authority themselves, that their aim, on the contrary, would be to help establish the authority and power of others, of the people, of whom they were still a part and for whom they were not the "M.P.s". They had to try to persuade the masses, but in a democratic way, without interfering in family or private matters, abstaining from any form of hegemonic pressure on others. "Being a member of a Revolutionary Committee", say the texts, "does not mean being given advantages or being protected, nor being sheltered from justice ... There is no place in the Revolutionary Committees for individual, tribal or other favouritism".

Such were the principles and theoretical guidelines of the role of this new élite. But how did the movement function

5 At this stage we will note that this latter function stands every chance of being at the root of the Revolutionary Committees' unpopularity. But we will come back to this aspect of the institution in more detail.

on the ground and day to day? And, to start with, who could become a member of a Revolutionary Committee?

In principle, any male or female citizen 18 or over (Libyan, Arab, or non-Arab) who felt the vocation, who believed in the ideas of the *Green Book* and who felt capable of setting the example of the "New Man" (with the exception, however, of those men and women who had had close ties with the old monarchic régime) could become a member of a Revolutionary Committee. According to these criteria, recruitment should not be selective, and in fact it was not, at least not at the beginning. Thereafter, and for some years now, a strict selection process was to preside over the admission of new members. It is no longer just anybody who can play at new élites. The fact is that in the beginning there were quite a few marginals, adventurers, even semi-delinquents, who were able to join the movement. But although this form of social integration, was probably beneficial for the individuals themselves[6], there were serious disappointments for the movement which was being set up and whose image, if not influence, was to suffer. A person close to the Leader described it as follows: "Before, we took anybody, even without training. Often with a very low level, and despite a little training given by the directors of the RCs, they didn't really understand the ideas of the revolution. And that was dangerous. But we very quickly organised a solid and very systematic training programme. We take children from revolutionary backgrounds, aged between 6 and 8, on visits to holiday-camps. Later, when they get to secondary school, we give them a 3-month course in summer as well as 2 weeks in the middle of the year. Then they can visit 5 to 6 different countries, and they are encouraged to learn a minimum of 3 languages. They are also trained in theory, history, and general culture. They practise music, sport, DIY etc. The first group trained like this (400 to 500) finished at the end of 1984. With the advantage of an entirely valid university level, they are thus capable of taking on any kind of responsibilities. Now, those who have come from this training can instruct others. Although they

---

6 And, to a certain extent, for society as a whole, since, for example, it channelled part of the young delinquent element.

still only represent 4 or 5% (in 1984) of the members of the RCs, it is clear that the latter will have fewer and fewer people who are not trained. So, by the quality of their theoretical and practical knowledge, the members of the Revolutionary Committees should become less and less guilty of the misdeeds such as the one attributed to them at the Libyan Embassy in London. In spite of everything, it must be recognised that the RCs do not affect the essence of the life of the country; their presence and their action remain without influence on the economy, the finances, the army – at least when the latter was still 'classic'.

As regards the ordinary workings of the committees, each of them receives its instructions directly from the "Head Office" (El Mathab), which is also where its members meet. There are no – or very few – horizontal links between the different committees. As for the members amongst themselves, their only link is that of their common task; besides, it is explicit that each man and woman keeps his or her original links (family, professional, religious, national etc).

The action of the Revolutionary Committees, we have indicated, is revolutionary in essence; it is to encourage the masses (in a population which is typically Mediterranean in character) to participate in the workings of power, and to take possession thereof[7]. But this ambition was rapidly to come up against indifference, apathy, passivity and even open hostility from all or part of the population. So, how could the principles of the *Green Book* – the decisions for which were, however, taken in the Basic Congresses, but which (such as the closing of the private businesses) were very unpopular in certain social groups – be applied just by democratic persuasion and without recourse to other types of measures which were more provocative and more authoritarian?

Having assessed the danger of the exhortative directives being exceeded, in particular the one regarding "revolutionary control", Ghadafi was to state repeatedly that it was not the vocation of the RCs to become authoritarian

---

7 In 1978 Ghadafi announced and explained it as follows: "It is the essential duty of the RCs to form popular committees of workers. They must wipe out exploitation, profit, gold and silver, the distinction between master and slave, the oppressive society, until the men of this country become equal, from the mosque to the popular committees, and to the grave".

bodies "ruling" in some way "in place of the masses". Thereafter, these committees were regularly called to order on the subject of the objective of exemplarity and by limiting their tendency to put pressure on the masses[8].

It is undeniable that in many cases the orders were neglected or ignored by the members of the committees. So RCs were often seen behaving like real agitators, setting themselves up as judges, and even executioners, not as the teachers or missionaries of the "Book". Where necessary, the Guide of the Revolution did not hesitate to apply strict sanctions on the guilty. This was the case, for example, in 1985, after the events in London, when RC elements "went over the heads of" the diplomatic staff, causing a serious and lasting crisis in political relations between the Jamahirya and Great Britain[9].

2. THE JAMAHIRYAN RANKS

More spectacular than the other new élites, particularly because of their work noticed outside the Jamahirya, the female Jamahiryan Guards form an élite which is both very noticeable and yet very little known. For although it is a characteristic of this élite group to willingly show itself in public, it is hardly spoken of; its role and its actions appear neither in the official discourse nor in the public speeches, whether for praise or caution.

When the Guide of the Libyan Revolution appeared surrounded by guards from the female corps – for the first time in Libya itself and then regularly on his subsequent trips abroad – the international press and television gave a large place to what was perceived as a new "craze" of the Colonel. Comments abounded and there was no lack of interpretations of all kinds, the most common in Europe

8 "I do not authorise the members of the Revolutionary Committees to interfere in the business of the Popular Committees unless in rare exceptions, as their mission is only revolutionary encouragement. But they must be capable of forcing the Popular Committees to carry out the decisions of the Basic Popular Congress and eradicate favouritism, hidden intermediaries, negligence and disorder from them." (speech of 23.4.1985 at Tripoli Town Council).

9 Contrary to the information published in the Western Press, several political members of the Popular Office (embassy) were severely punished on their return to Tripoli.

being to assimilate these bodyguards into a form of modern "harem".

During our sojourns in Libya we had the opportunity to meet several young women belonging to this group, particularly among those who had been part of Ghadafi's escort abroad. On the whole they were not very talkative (probably on instructions), but they did, however, provide us with some precise information regarding their training and their functions. The interview which follows summarises the main points:

Fariba (26) and Naima (24) – one very beautiful, the other favoured little by nature – had both been "guards" for several years already, and each had made several trips abroad with the Leader (so one had been, amongst other places, to Yugoslavia, the other to Malta and China). The first was a French language teacher in a secondary school, the second an officer in the army. Apart from the ordinary military training and their professional training itself, they had both gone through a special training, the same, or almost, they explained, as for their male colleagues.

The fact is, and this is not very well-known, the women guards are part of the same "corps", if we can say that, as the men; an élite corps, composed solely of volunteers. The training takes place over a longish period, at least several months. The officer Naima was able to do this training by taking part in daytime sessions, being released from her professional military obligations during this period. Fariba, on the other hand, as she could not free herself from her lessons, had to take part in evening training, which naturally lasted longer. Both periodically went through "maintenance" courses.

How and why had they become "guards"?
– "You should not look on us as a separate group; our motivations are the same as those of our male colleagues. The Guards represent the whole of the Jamahiryan population. The revolution concerns everybody, men and women. We must fight together for its success, until it is achieved. The presence of Female Guards confirms this; men and women are responsible together for the revolution and the life of Moammar El Ghadafi. As soon as people accept the revolution, it is logical that they protect it and that the first thing is

to protect the man who instigated it and guides it. Moammar's life is very important for all of us. So there are a lot of us who apply to join the guards. But obviously you have to meet certain selection criteria, the most important of which is to be physically capable. There are even children who apply sometimes, but of course they are not accepted."

– "No, physical beauty has nothing to do with it, not for men nor for women. But we are tested physically and psychologically, particularly for the speed of our reflexes. The girls, like the men, come from all areas of Libya, from all backgrounds, from all professions. All are volunteers and unpaid. There are several sections in the institution of the guards, in particular separate male and female sections."

– "No, Brother Moammar never chooses his guards himself; others do it for him. I can tell you how it happens for us. We receive a summons: 'Be at such and such a place at such and such a time.' If one girl is not available, another will go; but in principle you must always be available, as otherwise, you can't continue to be part of the Guards. When the meeting is in Tripoli itself, I go there in my own car; it's more convenient, and then I come straight back home" explained Naima. "And if it's outside, we are taken together". Fariba added: "When it's abroad, we are warned in advance. But we don't know what the exact destination is."

Why does Ghadafi surround himself especially with Female Guards?
– "It's because he wants to show the whole world that the revolution is for both sexes. And that he trusts women as much as, if not more than, men to protect him!"

– "The difference between the Guards and the Rahibat? We have nothing in common, except that we protect the whole revolution, we, physically, and the Rahibat, ideologically. But we keep a private life, whereas they give their whole lives to the revolution; they sacrifice themselves to it completely".

3. THE RELIGIOUS NUNS (Rahibat thawriya)

If the members of the RCs are an organisational instrument of the revolution, and if the women officers and the female guards incarnate a certain model of "liberated woman", the revolutionary nuns are to be regarded as a separate élite, the élite of the élites, whose qualitative superiority has been underlined by Ghadafi himself; "You will be the most revolutionary force and the one most in a position to stop the regression of the (Arab) Nation. It is you who will accomplish a historical mission[10]."

It was on 13 February 1981, during a meeting in Benghazi with the "pioneers of the female revolutionary formations" that the Colonel for the first time introduced the principle of the creation of a movement of "revolutionary nuns". He was then to mention it again on different occasions at meetings and military or civil congresses.

This revolutionary movement – at the service of the revolution, not religion – is in principle open to all women, civilians as well as soldiers. In reality, it is addressed to a minority, a very small minority, for the members of this "élite of the élites" must be ready to sacrifice their lives, their whole lives, exclusively to the aims of the revolution. They must give up any personal private life, as groups of men and women moved by the passion of serving an ideal have always done. Ghadafi explained himself on this subject in a speech given on 13 February 1981: "The movement of the revolutionary nuns doesn't date from today. Each age, each civilisation, has engendered a movement of religious fervour, and that existed before Islam and Christianity, before the Roman Empire and those before that. What does that mean? It does seem that a certain number of people have felt a strong need to stop their life to serve what is sacred for the nation, what is necessary for their civilisation, their beliefs, their lives themselves. These people stop everything to serve an ideal; God, Christ, the sacred fire, or any other target[11]".

Ghadafi referred explicitly to the Christian nuns "who dress in white, the symbol of purity, and who give themselves completely to the ideal of Christ", to exclaim: "Why do the Christians become nuns, and you stay sitting and watching? Does it mean that the Christian nuns are greater than the

---

10 Quotations taken from the book by H. Barrada, M. Kravetz and M. Whittaker: *Ghadafi: Je suis un opposant à l'échelon mondial*, Ed. Favre, 1984.
11 *Op. cit.*

Arab nation?" And he added: "It is in denial that the revolutionary nun is sacred and pure, and puts herself above ordinary individuals to be closer to the angels[12]".

By this appeal to "sacrifice", to the revolution, the renunciation of any private life and marriage, Ghadafi wants to make the image of being single lose any negative connotation. If being single in general, and in particular for women, is traditionally regarded as a situation which is against nature, indeed even anti-Islamic, Ghadafi strongly disputes this:

"Who tells you that marriage is compulsory in Islam? Each man and woman is free to marry or not to marry. Does God ask you for reasons for not getting married? Will you be threatened with hell for refusing marriage? On the contrary, you are more angels of purity!"

And he justifies the reasons for being single so:

"Marriage places responsibilities on other people, it leads to successive problems. What value does (traditional) marriage have today? You study for a diploma to, in the end, give yourselves to a nobody, who only sees in you a maid, a cook, and a breeding-machine, and who disclaims you for a 'yes' or a 'no', without regard for your university diploma, without respect for your participation in the revolution . . . Do you accept this situation or not? If 5% don't accept this situation for themselves, I wouldn't wish for anything more[13]".

So, what role is devolved to this new élite? It is a role of provocation and challenge, a role of ideological and moral avant-garde "to liberate the masses who are now still outside humanity". But it is not a role of power; unlike some religious organisations, which get involved in politics and which seek power – like the Moslem Brotherhood – the movement of the revolutionary nuns has no connection, Ghadafi states, with "the power which is in the hands of the people". They are therefore called on to work "to consolidate the revolutionary power of the people, to destroy the old society, and to burn the filth which infests the Arab nation. For the Arab nation today needs a movement of

12 Speech 13 February 1981.
13 Speech 13 February 1981.

revolutionary nuns totally devoted to the revolution to put an end to reaction, Zionism, the Crusades, divisions, and to set up socialism, progress and Arab unity . . . A movement which is capable of stopping the regression of the Arab nation".

Having had the opportunity to notice "revolutionary nuns" (rahibat thawriya) in different professional environments (administration, education, hospitals, the army), we requested an interview with three of them. Through the opinions obtained, we can discern a certain view of the way in which they themselves see their role and their commitment, and in which they live their situation from day to day.

The interview presented here is with a woman professor of one of the Libyan universities. Miriam was 29; she came from a large family; her father was a modest civil servant in the administration. She taught chemistry and physics, and enlisted as a "rahibat" as early as 1981, that is at the first appeal from Colonel Ghadafi, when the movement was formed.

"I was still a student at the Science Faculty and I had already been a member of a revolutionary committee for some time. I thought the ideas of our revolution were very beautiful, particularly concerning the liberation of women, and I fought for them. When the Leader suggested creating the movement of the 'rahibat', I was immediately convinced that this was a more effective way, and I joined.

The commitment is mainly a personal matter, a personal promise; you promise to give yourself completely to the revolution and to sacrifice your private life, particularly marriage and making a home. All the same, it doesn't mean that we leave our families and our friends, we keep a certain availability for them, but they are no longer a priority.

We follow lessons and we meet regularly to exchange our ideas and our experiences. We, the rahibat, are like the Christian nuns, but instead of giving our lives to religion (like they do to Christ) we give ourselves completely to the ideas of the revolution. The rahibat has nothing to do with religion as such. I am a Moslem and I am a strong believer, but religion, for me, is a personal matter, a matter between myself and God.

To accomplish revolution and liberation in society, to fight against imperialism and Zionism, it is necessary to be united. Women must take part in all this as much as men. If in every Arab country there are a thousand women or more who, remaining single, give themselves completely to the revolution, then we can have a real influence and succeed in changing things.

Arab women aren't yet capable of defending themselves, they are not at all liberated, and this liberation must come from the Arab countries themselves, not from America or Europe.

The most difficult thing is to influence men. Arab men are 'asleep'. They think that everything is wonderful. They are not aware of the situation, and especially not of the position of women. There are already men who are liberated, but there aren't many of them – the majority aren't yet liberated, they aren't up to it.

Why do we promise to stay single? For a woman, getting married today still means being a slave at home. That is why we don't want to get married. Once I was married, I wouldn't have any more time. I would have too much to do in the family and at home, even if my husband helped me a bit.

First we have to work at liberating people by educating them and explaining to them how we can become free according to the ideas of the *Green Book*. We have to fight for this both in our country and in the other Arab countries and even outside. That's why I joined!

No, my family weren't enthusiastic at the beginning – my father even thought the idea was absurd. For my parents, a woman who isn't married is unthinkable, she isn't a real woman. Even though my father was agreeable to my studying science, he thought that my destiny was to become a wife and mother. Studies, for him, were more a general culture and a useful pastime than a future profession. I tried explaining to him that our revolution, with which he is in complete agreement, also means a change in mentality, and that it is necessary for a certain number of men and women to give themselves exclusively to it. My family nevertheless remained quite sceptical. But when you want to be a 'rahibat', you must be strong, impossible to influence, and above criticism. And now that, for almost 9 years, I have kept my promise, they respect me and they understand me better. It is also true that Libyan society has started to change in the meantime and that people have got used to these new and different ideas. We, the young, have studied the *Green Book* a lot at school, at university and in the committees; and we often discuss things together. For the old generation, it's more difficult, they have been brought up differently.

Why, as a rahibat, do I still carry on my professional life? It's because science is very important and necessary for the revolution. As a teacher, I can also bear witness as a revolutionary and a liberated woman. Besides, everything I do must express my options!

But, in fact, not all the rahibats work. Those who don't have any income are kept by their committees.

In principle, men can commit themselves in the same way; it's a purely personal commitment".

Other questions were asked, to which it has remained impossible for us to get even an approximate answer. Were there many in the Jamahirya of today who had opted for this path, or were women like Miriam an exception? Did they really keep their promise, for life? Nothing, in truth, helped to enlighten us on the number of rahibats, even less so on the number of those who might have abandoned the movement en route, nor on the extent of their commitment.

Although each of the élite groups described above has, we have seen, its own characteristics, they have in common the fact that they are élites of influence and not élites of power; these élites of influence are crystallised around ideologies, taking part in defining and publicising them. Communicating the ideas of the revolution by influence (and not by the exercise of power) is indeed the main aim assigned to them. Each does this according to different tactics and with varying degrees of effectiveness. So the movement of the Revolutionary Committees has, in theory at least, the task of being the educating and organising instrument of the revolution; the women officers must represent firstly the model of the "liberated woman" in Libyan society. The Jamahiryan Guards are also a model of liberated women but are supposed, just by their physical presence in a precise context, to communicate the revolutionary message that men and women are equal in value in the revolution, a message which, despite being obvious, is often interpreted wrongly in the West: instead of the "liberated protective angel", they become "exploited harem women". Finally, the revolutionary nuns go further, having to incarnate the very spirit of the revolution by being in some way the living symbols of a way of thinking, of being, of acting. They have to provoke both imitation and identification. They are likely to exercise an influence and to contribute to the social change by the value of the exemplary behaviour that they incarnate.

Is this influence of a minority élite effective? It is impossible to answer this question directly. These élites appear to present characteristics that can be regarded as useful to the exercise of a social influence; above all, a high degree of certainty regarding their own judgements. Feeling competent and stronger than others, they have a specific style of behaviour which expresses both the desire to influence others and that of resistance to others. Their attitude is neither dominating nor inclined to compromise, and denotes a certain autonomy with regard to institutions as well as persons.

Chapter V

A global strategy
to change mentalities

Often described as unpredictable, Moammar el Ghadafi is especially so in his tactical style. His ideological options appear certain in their strategic consistency and relatively clear. On the other hand, the Guide of the Revolution is in the habit of varying the use of his tactics – and this often makes perception of the elements of prediction difficult. Nonetheless, we can identify a certain number of principles in his behaviour.

Ghadafi's ideology aims explicitly at overthrowing an old order and establishing a new society by seeking particular models and creating institutions which conform to his vision of modern Libya. It expresses a desire to construct a different social and human world. What resources does Ghadafi choose to employ to carry out his plans?

Above all, he declares that he relies on the human will: "It is man's will which is the fundamental factor in the movement of history; and it is thanks to it that the mass society can be founded, the governmental and class institutions destroyed, the system of salaries abolished, society on the basis of partnership achieved, and the State of the Masses

– the Jamahirya – set up". Later he was to declare: "If conviction is not enough, it will be by provocation and force" (speech, 1978).

So, from the declamations' point of view, Ghadafi favours the role of individual and collective effort, which includes the use of force, but apparently only retains a part limited to outside conditions. Nevertheless, he certainly does not stop himself from exploiting these, thus adopting a position aiming classically to transform an unfavourable circumstance into a favourable one. For example, when the reduction in oil revenue was to force Libya to adopt a strict economic policy, Ghadafi was to emphasise the necessity of increasing production and producing on the scale of what they wanted to consume. At first, he would use this to explain the necessity of integrating women – they represent 50% of the potential active adult population – into a global project for economic and social planning. In a second stage, after noticing the danger into which the Jamahirya would run through its transformation into a Western-style consumer society, he was to seize the first opportunity to provoke a largely artificial shortage in supplies.

The ideology of the equality of the sexes was here used to the benefit of the needs of the production apparatus, and vice versa. By seizing opportunities which are offered, Ghadafi uses the promotion of equality between men and women as a means to establish, by the formation of a base extended to both sexes, a democracy in which the notion of universal integrates the two sexes.

Unlike other reformers (whether Islamic or not), Ghadafi, with an ideological aim, applies forms of positive discrimination, favouring the adoption of measures advantageous to categories which are vulnerable or in a position of weakness[1]. So, in the event of divorce, Libyan women are entitled to keep the house for their benefit.

1 In 1986 the amendment of the French electoral code which fixed the contingent of women on the lists of candidates at a minimum of 25% was declared unconstitutional by reason of the Declaration on the Rights of Man, which stipulates equality between the sexes. Unesco, for its part, regards positive discrimination quite differently, judging in Article 4 of its Charter that: "the adoption by States of special temporary measures aiming to accelerate the establishment of de facto equality between men and women is not regarded as an act of discrimination".

Prompt to seize on the opportunities in this domain, the Guide of the Revolution also knows how to create them; for example, by playing with the mental habits inherited from custom. Notwithstanding his openly declared preference for "co-education", therefore the abolition of the traditional "infical", from 1985 he reintroduced this notion of "infical" into the organisation of the Basic Congresses in order to help strengthen the female presence in the People's General Congress. For despite a not insignificant participation in the Basic Congresses (in the order of 15 to 20%), women were and still are very rarely appointed for the executive bodies and even less as spokeswomen at the General Congress. One way of changing this situation was thus to create female Basic Congresses, by reintroducing the rule of infical. By doing this, Ghadafi gave priority to tactics over his declared ideological convictions[2].

More widely, as a social actor, the Guide of the Revolution has to remain – and he is forced to – in symbiosis with his environment. With keen knowledge of the mentalities of his people[3], he never fails to refer to the basic values of his own society. Is he led to break off with the immediate past? He takes care, immediately and as if by compensation, to go back to an old fundamental past to target the idealised future of an egalitarian society, fair for all. In this way, each time he intends to introduce any social innovation, he refers explicitly either to religion ("It is in denial that the revolutionary nun is sacred, pure, above ordinary individuals and closer to the angels"), or to the traditions of the Arab society ("The presence of women on palanquins who used to accompany men going to war represented a gesture of defiance and provocation, in the same way as the movement of the revolutionary women does today").

As we have previously emphasised, Ghadafi tries to rely on a minimum consensus of common values to make possible

---

2 If this tactic were pushed to its extreme, the People's General Congress would become the first political institution in the world where men and women were equal in number.

3 A fact which observers have too often a tendency to underestimate. But, in the other direction, in many circumstances we have been able to identify a real difficulty on his part to understand the attitude and the reactions of the Western world with regard to him.

Participant at the Basal Congress

and facilitate communication with his fellow citizens. His
heretical discourse aims not only at shattering adherence to
the universe of the common understanding, by publicly
professing the break with the burdens of the norms and
the ordinary order, but also at producing a new common
understanding, so as to include the practices and the tacit or
repressed experiences of a whole group.

Among new ideas which are really revolutionary in the
Arab-Moslem context, the Ghadafian ideology, because of
the past that it calls on, carries with it typically traditionalist
elements (history, religion and customs). In this, his behaviour tallies with that of many other heads of state, political

Popular Theatre

men or social actors of any ideology. Is it through conviction, or through a desire to preserve a cognitive coherence? "There is in him a resolve to get to the essence and to pursue logical reasoning to the end", noted J. P. Charvin[4]. Sometimes he pushes his reasoning as such even to the absurd so as to better show up the shallowness or the inconsistency in the behaviour of those he is speaking to. A humorous example of this is given in one of his speeches related to the opponents and revolutionaries of the world[5]. Neither does he hesitate to attack traditionalist Moslems,

4 J. P. Charvin and J. Vignet-Zunz, *Le syndrome Kadhafi*, Editions Albatros, 1987.
    5 Speech 1/83 in Tripoli, quoted in: *Kadhafi, je suis un opposant . . . (op. cit. p. 173)*.

165

whom he reproaches for not being strict enough: "They take a whole verse from the Qu'ran, or a part, and they interpret it in their own way without taking account of the context, what goes before it and what follows".

Under the Ghadafian discourse lies a concept of society whose presentation has systematic recourse to history. In so doing, he often seems to have no other aim than to suggest a certain permanence. Without doubt this apparent concern for roots and ideological continuity by the reinterpretation of traditions also demonstrates in Ghadafi a profound rejection of the patriarchal heritage. Where some of his predecessors in Islamic reformism (Ataturk, Reza Shah) had directly attacked sacred symbols, such as the wearing of the veil or the institutions of the dowry and the mahr, Ghadafi seems more to be trying over a long period to cautiously dismantle the social institution which is judged archaic.

In this sense, one would be tempted to describe his strategy as reformist and evolutionist rather than revolutionary. The choice of such prudent tactical options is also confirmed in other different areas; for example, that of agricultural development, where we have very often observed the co-existence of traditional agriculture and animal-keeping with ultra-modern agricultural enterprises using avant-garde techniques (irrigation, management by computer).

In any case, we can see that Ghadafi has not ceased to take public opinion into account. On the subject of women working, for example, for a long time he defended the principle of their specific nature, slotting active women into socio-professional areas generally regarded by the population as more "acceptable", more "female" (health and education in particular). Should we see in that the reflection of an ideological conviction which was later modified? Or a political calculation aiming to facilitate the integration of women into the workforce? It was by the creation of the model of the woman at arms, in 1979, that he seemed to have clearly distanced himself from the "principles", to adopt an open tactic of provocation and challenge, by inviting women to preach an example.

In fact, social change, in Libya as elsewhere, finds an

important source of energy in opposition to the existing order; it is precisely in controversy that forms of social renewal are most often expressed. If Ghadafi only assigned himself this role late, after developing his political reflection and diversifying his experiences, it was also because he could not practise it at the time of the *coup d'état*.

Unknown in his country, he first of all had to be accepted and recognised as a charismatic leader, providing inspiration at the same time as serving as a symbol to the movement. He had to acquire the trust and the respect of those close to him and those of the popular masses so as to have an accumulated credit, allowing him to question the existing norms and to promote fundamental changes. Quite naturally, he was therefore led to look for the best way, the best method of demonstration and representation to express the aspirations of certain groups of population whose energies he tried to channel towards a target predetermined by him; this applies in particular to his major social project, the creation of a new society in the form of an egalitarian "State of the Masses". His strategy regarding the advancement of women was no different.

By dismantling the patriarchate and its way of thinking at the base, Ghadafi is trying to supplant the old social categories with new ones. But this substitution does not operate without a change, powerfully controlled, in the practices and the rules. By the lasting use and respect of them, these new categories of thinking are constructed and a new set of imaginary and mobilising representations is elaborated[6].

The choice to establish the Women's Military Academy as the spearhead of change was a gamble, for as soon as women are forced towards practices and rules which upset the image that they have of themselves, they find themselves directly confronted with the traditional representations of men. A condition of success for this gamble lay in the maintenance of cohesion in the social forces mobilised by the change. So, if we refer to the theory of social action developed by M. van Bockstaele and P. Schein: "{The}

6 Maria van Bockstaele and Pierrette Schein: "Limites des négociations et négociations des limites", *Sociologie du travail*, Paris, January–March 1972.

representations capable of maintaining the cohesion of the social forces are upheld by practices and their symbolic transcription; through the deeply impregnated marks of the value of the goals, through the ritual of the acts, through the rules which order {individuals}, the sacred pole of the project is maintained, the one which bears the imaginary representations and the Utopian images[7].

The leading power is responsible for seeing to the maintenance of this sacred pole which it symbolises. It has to attract available energies by operating a transfer towards this new set of imaginary and mobilising representations; it thus brings the myth and the social Utopia up to date: "Any reformatory or revolutionary effort attacks this transferential zone by trying to develop or on the contrary to destroy the legitimacy of the bases of these representations[8]".

But to change the bases assumes that one knows them and takes them into account. Ghadafi knows the traditional society well, including its strongest rules, the most symbolic of which concern the relationships between men and women. He knows that by attacking this problem he is touching on the heart of the social system. He knows that the women's mentality cannot be changed without also modifying the men's: "This presence of the project of the other within the project of the one manifests itself on several levels of interaction. The actors represent all the elements which in their eyes constitute the project or projects of the other actors in the negative, in complement or in correspondence to their actions . . . No project can be constituted outside this field of interaction[9].

This double, encased project on the one hand grasps the opposition between traditional society and modernist society, and on the other favours the advancement of women as a lever to act on this opposition. To conduct such an action, hazards must be anticipated and managed carefully just as much as stability.

In fact, the complexity of this project which was running against the tide was only going to reveal itself little by little.

7 *Op. cit., p. 22.*
8 *Op. cit., p. 24.*
9 *Op. cit., p. 21.*

The Ghadafian discourse of the first few years adopted a proleptic form[10], that is, a systematic search for answers which were based on questions or objections not yet formulated but which it was felt would arise. The difference between the anticipations explicitly formulated and the results noted can be a resource if it is detected, evaluated and used correctly. Its attentive management generates the movement and the mobilisation of forces in uncertain situations.

No important innovation is possible if it does not exercise its energy from the top to the bottom of the social ladder. Ghadafi seems to know intuitively that minority discourse draws its sense from the position of the person giving it as much as from what he is expressing. Once he had been accepted as "leader", it became possible for him to distance himself from the majority opinions, to start on his role as challenger of the existing institutions, in short to announce an innovative deviation.

By playing on the minority-majority relationships, he found, for his action, a new anchorage directly from the opposition between the modernist society and the traditional society. The first thing any innovator has to do is to attract attention to himself; isn't one of the major handicaps to his influence inattention and indifference, producing incredibility? Whether he is thought to be a nice person or not, a social irregular claiming to be a founder must intrigue, interest and provoke if he does not want to lose any potential ascendancy. Non-conformist, but accepted and recognised as Leader and President, Ghadafi was able to establish himself relatively quickly; the affirmation of self, the autonomy of behaviour, the desire to force recalcitrant destiny would do the rest. The size of the Libyan nation was certainly an important factor, but this factor is not an explanation in itself. It seems that Ghadafi has been able to decipher the basic contradictions of Libyan society in order to propose new solutions. From there, he would become more and more an image-symbol, a source of ambiguous attitudes, attractive and repulsive in nature, including for those whose social destiny he intended to question, directly or not, inside as well as outside the country. Aware of the sanctions or censures that his schemes

10 *Op. cit., p. 20.*

arouse, especially abroad, he declares himself to be determined to assume the consequences[11]. But in return, this blatant non-conformism also attracts him a certain regard, sometimes even from those who show themselves to be the most hostile to his policy.

Having often succeeded in putting others in the position of looking for reasons for his behaviour, he has managed to provoke a sort of "brainstorming" in and on the subject of Libyan society, leading his interlocutors to imagine different solutions, to conceive possible perspectives outside the ways traditionally proposed or imposed. In certain favourable cases, the perception of an alternative will *ipso facto* trigger an intellectual effort to perceive, understand and measure the potential consequences of the proposed innovation[12].

Following on from his speeches and his acts, this activity of imagining perspectives of change and modalities of action, an activity of imagination used with regard to society, constitutes the bedrock of the sociological transfer: "The power to change the bases {of the} representations of the real and to induce imaginary representations and Utopian images mobilising social forces gets mixed up with the ability to provoke the sociological transfer[13]."

Ghadafi keeps this sociological transfer bubbling by changing the supports to which he adheres. Having become an "opponent" – as he was later to proclaim himself[14] – could

11 See the TF1 programme: "Face au Public", 29 February 1984. In reply to a French journalist who questioned him on the feelings that he felt personally when he was accused of being a terrorist, the Colonel declared:
    Question: "Colonel, you are sitting in the dock; but behind your politician's shell, does your personal sensibility feel affected by all the evils of which you are accused?"
    Ghadafi: "That's a deduction, not a question, but I can congratulate you on this good deduction. I can't answer".
    Question: "But how do you feel about this criticism?[11]"
    Ghadafi: "What is important is the 'motivations', the motivations that are behind these accusations. Consequently, if it's the truth, well then I accept my responsibilities and I try to live *my* truth".

12 In 1985, the whole of Tripoli was shaken by the proposals of the Colonel and his team regarding the possible introduction of education at home by the parents themselves, from the first year of primary school. And the discussions were going on everywhere, particularly in female circles.

13 *Op. cit., p.* 24.

14 *Je suis un opposant à l'échelon mondial.* Interviews with Hamid Barrada, Marc Kravetz and Marc Whittaker, Editions Fabre, 1985.

Ghadafi continue to exercise apparent formal power? A power whose purpose could certainly consist of modifying the existing state of things, but whose first function was to keep the edifice in balance, not to upset the social institutions from top to bottom.

Ghadafi had tried to gamble on this risk in 1978 when he decided to resign from power and give himself the role of Guide of the Revolution. On the occasion of the 9th anniversary of the coup d'état of 1 September 1969, he had already declared: "Power and the revolution have to be separated. I will no longer exercise power but I will practise the revolution with the revolutionary forces. I will get back my true place, which is in the revolution and not in power. As soon as the people assume their responsibilities, they become their own government. From then on, it is I who am in opposition". Ghadafi would repeat this challenge in other forms until that day in March 1988 when, in front of the People's General Congress, he was to announce his intention to open the gates of all the Libyan prisons![15]

Did he ever really leave administrative power, day-to-day power?

Officially, having ceased to be "President" in 1978, he no longer deals with the running of the State. In reality, he continues to exercise his powers through two bodies: that of the "technocrats" in the régime, a lobby which was often more obliging than ideologised; and that of the new revolutionary élites. By a very knowing slalom, acting on these "two wheels" of the revolution[16], Ghadafi

---

15 Speech of 3 March 1988, on the occasion of the opening of the prisons and the destruction of the one in Tripoli (which he undertook himself, against the wish of certain groups of Libyans). He declared in particular: "I am the first opponent in the world" (but also in Libya!).

16 Somebody close to the régime in 1984 presented to us, in image form, his theory of Ghadafian power.

According to this theory of the "two wheels", the practice of power in Libya would put in the centre two parallel forces of energy; the revolutionaries, on the one hand, and the technocrats on the other. The revolutionaries are moved spontaneously by the suggestions or proposals of the Guide. As executors, they sometimes act too quickly, and too blindly. This wheel is for all that the dynamic element, the real engine of the revolution, which sometimes has to be braked or re-centred.

The technocrats, financiers and administrators do not deal very much with policy. But they are essential for designing and carrying out the projects, particularly in the area of development. *cont.*

171

has widely shown his political agility and his qualities as a manoeuvrer[17].

It remains for the effectiveness of this strategy to be assessed, applied to the change in mentalities within the young generation. This will be the subject of the third and final part of this work. But before starting this section, there is still one question to be asked; how far forward, from strategy to tactical choices, can the Leader of the Libyan Revolution go? Are all means good for him? Or does he impose some limits on his action, and which ones?

Here we touch on the case of terrorism brought against Ghadafi's Libya by the West, a case which comes back to posing, through mutual mystifications, the question of the tactical choices made by the Guide of the Revolution for his external action, but also and firstly the legitimacy of the action itself on an international level.

Ghadafi does not allow withdrawal into inside the national borders. He regards the values of his ideology as universal and he addresses all men on earth. Logically, this ambition gives him permission to take up a stance and to act both inside his own country – and even in opposition to the Jamahirya which he has created[18] – and outside, on an international level. In his speeches, the rejection of injustice is radical, whether that practised on women by the patriarchal system, or that practised on peoples by neo-colonialism

16. cont. The Guide sometimes relies on one group, sometimes on the other. So the two wheels, although independent, are both essential to move the revolution forward.

It is because at the beginning it had neglected the second wheel, and let the first turn too freely, that – according to this speaker – the Libyan revolution had met with breakdowns and even skids on its own circuit.

17 We should emphasise that Ghadafi's interest in strategic games is old and constant. During an interview conducted by Mirella Bianca (*Kadhafi, messager du désert*, 1974, p. 146), the Colonel expressed himself as follows on the preparations for the 1 September revolution: "From the point of view that our revolution was going to be a popular revolution, any revolutionary experience could be useful to us and would deserve study. It wasn't the substance, the ideological content, which interested us; but the method in which it had been carried out, its practical side, its technique in short".

18 In March 1988, Ghadafi violently accused his fellow citizens of turning their "Jamahirya" into a prison, for example by requiring exit visas from their own people, and in the same way by imposing a male authorisation for women to travel. On this occasion, he was to himself tear up the required forms in public.

and imperialism[19]. This leads not only to taking up positions in favour of those that he regards as "oppressed", but also actions intended to give justice, to redress the wrongs (and this just as much on behalf of Palestinians or Arab women as Irish Catholics and English dockers): "I stand by the side of revolutionary opposition, by the side of the man in the street, the persecuted man, whether Christian or Moslem". In his view this desire (or, if you like, this vocation) to build a different social and human world does not want to and cannot know any impediments or any frontiers.

He does not deny that these schemes and these actions permit the use of violence, and justify it; as a "true" Moslem, he invokes the principles of an Islam which legitimises recourse to violence for the purpose of establishing justice, a justice which is given priority in a relationship where peace is only to be regarded as a factor in justice, not as an instrument of reconciliation and temporary understanding. If the "jihad" can sublimate itself in a personal effort, a struggle against oneself, to arrive at supreme transcendency and well-being, this word has remained and still remains synonymous with "just war", justifying the use of violence[20].

According to this logic, it becomes obvious that Ghadafi's Libya subsidises and provides preparation, training and arms for numerous opposition groups, and that in certain cases it even takes part directly in armed action (the Palestinian revolt in Lebanon for example). The Colonel does not defend himself for this. Rather he boasts of it, as, according to what he declared: "This support for just causes was a noble act on the part of Libya"[21].

But, in the same interview, and just as explicitly, he ruled out the possibility of co-operation with terrorist organisations such as the Red Brigade "who only represent a cry of revolt and do not constitute a reasonable and acceptable opposition for society". "One understands", he went on to say, "the psychological, social, even political motivations of their members; but one cannot agree with

19 He draws this parallel on several occasions, comparing, for example, the Arab family to a colonised people.
20 Cf. J. P. Charnay (in: *L'Islam et la guerre*, Ed. Fayard, 1986, p. 229).
21 Cf. H. Barrada, *Op cit.*

173

their methods, which are to be condemned". Here Ghadafi stated that he rejected "blind terrorism"[22].

It seems that from these and other declarations we can draw the at least provisional conclusion that the Guide of the Libyan Revolution in effect imposes moral limits on himself, even though these limits do not necessarily correspond to legal norms defined by national or international bodies. On this subject we will quote a passage from an article by Claude Julien, written after the assassination of Jean-Marie Tjibaou in June 1989: "Everybody knows the eternal boundary between the'good' and the 'bad' terrorists. The former are designated by their political victory, the second by their defeat, until the day when a new relationship of the forces reverses the roles. Their weapons and their methods, however, are identical . . . Who, therefore, will decide that the right to a fatherland justifies violence in one case, and condemns it in another?[23]

22 This corresponds with "the confession" of a close collaborator of Ghadafi during a private interview: "Since the IRA started throwing bombs on buses and hotels, we haven't financed them any more" (June 1988). We should also point out that in 1978 Libya became party to the international agreement on terrorism in the area of civil aviation. It is well known that since this date no aeroplane hijacked in flight has been given permission to land on Libyan territory. It also seems that no hijacker has been able to find refuge there.

23 Claude Julien "Respect", in *Le Monde Diplomatique*, June 1989.

PART III

EMPIRICAL STUDY OF THE DEVELOPMENT OF DEVELOPMENT OF MENTALITIES IN THE YOUNG GENERATION IN LIBYA DATA AND INTERPRETATIONS

Can we assess the impact of the new ideology among the young generation in Libya? And in particular, can we measure the differential impact of this ideology as regards women? Can we go so far as to speak of "Jamahiryan feminism"?

Studying the change involves analysing points of confrontation and their models in competition. This means trying to assess the influence of the new guiding images (in this case those of the Jamahiryan doctrine) at the points where they come into direct conflict with the old model (that is the patriarchate)[1].

It has often been assumed and stated that tradition and modernity are opposed to each other, that they necessarily conflict in all aspects, even that they are mutually exclusive[2]. This theory may be valid for certain societies in a decolonisation situation, where the colonial power had to be balanced, if not overturned, but it seems far too simplistic for the Libyan society of today.

In Libya, where those in charge are aiming to pass from one social and moral system to another in a single generation, it clearly seems that the process is not unwinding in a straight line. We find quite widespread interaction between the two systems. Certain elements of tradition can, by adapting, co-exist with the new social structure, even also become factors likely to induce change. The same applies to the traditional solidarity of the extended family, which, we have seen, helps

1 In reality the situation turned out to be more complex. In particular we noted two trends among the "female progressives"; one "Jamahiryan", the other closer to Western-style feminism. We will return to this point later.

2 J. Berque, for example, does not hesitate to stress the confrontation between the "qadim" (the old) and the "jadid" (the new), as in Les Arabes d'hier à demain.

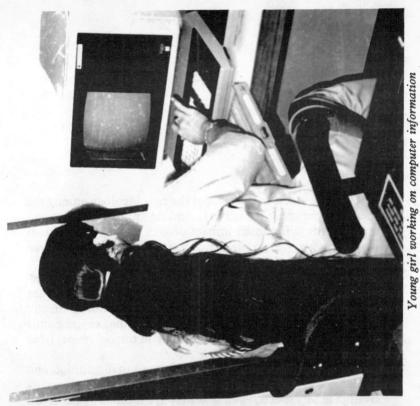

Young girl working on computer information

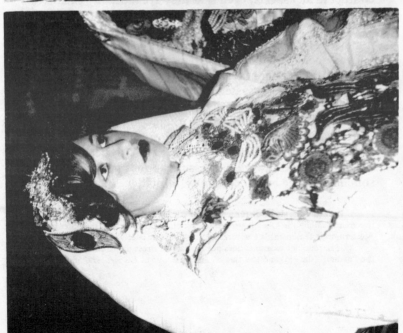

A female judge getting married in traditional dress

women to have independent work. Libya offers an example of a search for synthesis between traditional symbols and imagined modernity, a search which borrows from different origins (generally from outside the West) but does not exclude elements from its own history. Ghadafi reinterprets certain traditions as much as he rejects others. Here there is no uniform movement of rejection or borrowing; the social change is neither a total negation of the past nor an unconditional admiration for and reproduction of the modernity of others[3].

Nevertheless, some new references find themselves in direct conflict with those of the past; such is the case for the values affecting relationships between the sexes, in particular those attacking the traditional status of the father. As the family continues to be regarded as the basic unit of society, if an individual judges himself as liberated, he does not think that he ceases to be a member of this fundamental institution. It is therefore the whole collectivity that they must want to "liberate" and improve in quality, so as to remedy, through the equality of all its members, the situation of disparity inherited from the patriarchate. According to this theory, the emergence of the individual – and of a certain individualism – is therefore not incompatible with the maintenance of the family (or the collectivity) as the basis of society as a whole[4].

In order to assess the changes taking place in the structure of the Libyan family, and in the male and female roles in the collectivity, particularly relationships firstly between father and daughter, and then between husband and wife within the couple, we designed an observational tool presenting a dozen conflictual (for women) situations and asking the interviewees (men and women) to choose from several precoded answers.

The proposed answers gave a choice between two or sometimes three attitudes:

– submission and sacrifice on the part of the woman (to the parents, husband, the interests and needs of the family

3 On this subject see the individual interviews with the students of the WMA (Part II, Chapter II).

4 A theory which is, moreover, subject to controversy; cf. Mahmoud Hussein: *Versant sud de la liberté, essai de l'émergence de l'individu dans le tiers monde*, Ed. La Découverte, 1989.

group, the traditions and customs) by giving up her own ambitions (career, individual fulfilment etc): the traditionalist solution;

– the imposition of her will and her own interests and convictions (by disobedience, denial of the traditional "they say", sometimes sacrificing the collective interest); an attitude presented as "progressist": the modernist solution;

– in certain cases, the proposed answer contained a compromise solution by the use of possible sources of assistance (family, nursery, husband) for the woman to enter the world of work, for her personal fulfilment and her social promotion.

In this questionnaire we also included a few questions about the division of tasks between husband and wife in the home, so as to better outline the development of roles in this area, some seeming to change particularly quickly, especially since paid domestic work was abolished in Libya.

The definition of a particular role is based on a certain agreement embracing expectations on the part of other people. These expectations can be contradictory depending on the people or the environment[5]. Traditionally, a social role comprises the tasks and behaviour of an individual dictated by the status which he occupies. Any social apprenticeship, any interaction of relationships refers firstly to the status and role systems of the family environment (which is in its turn in relation to the surrounding society), and particularly those relating to age and sex. Then other influences will shape new terms of reference; in Libya, in particular, the Jamahiryan ideology communicated by the mass media and the schools. That is why we put together a sample made up of young people (17 to 30), all students, all brought up in Libyan families which were still on the traditional side, all having been subjected to the influence of the *Green Book* as well as the teaching of the Qu'ran.

Here we only wanted to examine the choices linked to the roles prescribed (by ideology, by tradition, or by religion).

Our first hypothesis is on the one hand that we must

5 On this subject see Part II, Chapter III, the illustration of some conflict situations.

expect a minimum consensus for the whole sample as regards the new values, and on the other that the individuals who were at the basis of this consensus – positive or negative in relation to the new values – refer either to one or another of the ideologies, marking their definition of a given role in this or that concrete situation. By that we also hoped that the measuring instrument would help us both to do a kind of status report on the transitory situation, and to understand the dynamics of change in mentalities in order to discern some probable evolutionary perspectives.

The second hypothesis, which deals with the results within each of the four groups, is that, depending on the degree of exposure to the influence of the new ideology, we would find significant differences between the groups.

An additional enquiry concerned the possible influence of the interviewees' background, defined by the social indicator "father's level of education".

Finally, the measuring instrument should be able to provide us with certain indications of the possible lags between concepts of the male and female roles (on the part of both sexes), which could possibly compromise the new adjustment.

It goes without saying that this measuring instrument has no normative value; at this stage it can only give comparative indications of trends.

Chapter I

The observation instrument

We gave preference to a study of the type: "What must a woman do in such or such a situation?" rather than direct or indirect observations on real behaviour, which would necessarily be distanced from the theoretical role.

Before analysing the results, some further information has to be given regarding the composition of the sample, the structure of the observation instrument, and the difficulties in interpreting and classifying the answers.

1 DESCRIPTION OF THE FOUR GROUPS STUDIED

The whole sample consisted of 183 young men and women, aged between 17 and 30 (average age 22), all students. According to the subjects they were studying, they can be divided as follows:

– 50 female students from the El Fatah University in Tripoli[1];

– 50 male students from the same university;

1 The male and female students questioned belonged to the following faculties: Arts, Law, Philosophy, Economics and Science.

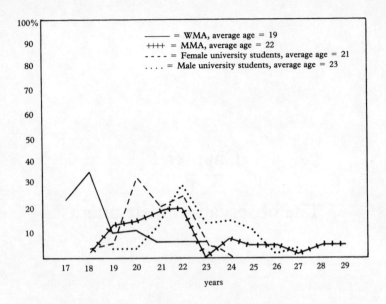

——— = WMA, average age = 19
++++ = MMA, average age = 22
- - - - = Female university students, average age = 21
.... = Male university students, average age = 23

years

– 46 men student officers (MMA);
– 33 women student officers (WMA);
i.e. a total of 179 questionnaires duly completed (four were incomplete as they had been moved away).

We adopted the father's level of education as the "social indicator" of the background, and divided it into three categories: (1) illiterate or almost; (2) primary school or a few years more; (3) baccalaureat or higher.

The division for the whole sample was as follows: (1) illiterate father 22%; (2) primary and above 56%; (3) bac and above 22%.

Three of the four groups in the sample were very close to this average; the WMA, the female university students and the male university students. The fourth group, the MMA, came from slightly less well educated backgrounds; one-third had fathers who were illiterate; only 11% of the male student officers' fathers had the bac (only one had been to university)[2].

2 Contrary to an opinion quite common in Libyan society, the female officers more often belong to educated families; 28% of them had fathers with the bac or university level.

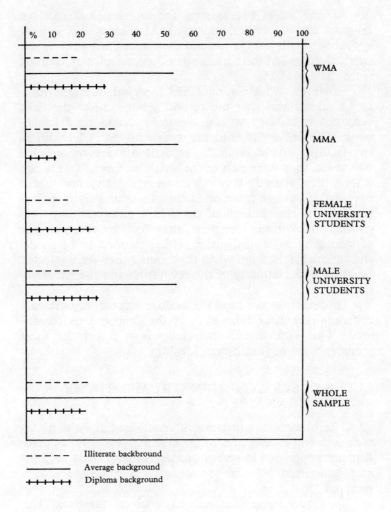

| % | 10 | 20 | 30 | 40 | 50 | 60 | 70 | 80 | 90 | 100 |

WMA

MMA

FEMALE
UNIVERSITY
STUDENTS

MALE
UNIVERSITY
STUDENTS

WHOLE
SAMPLE

– – – – – Illiterate backbround
─────── Average background
+++++++ Diploma background

The table above gives the percentages by category for each of the four groups and for the whole sample.

As for age, the women were generally a little younger than the men, and among them the students from the WMA were the youngest:

185

All the interviewees, men and women, had received religious and ideological education. At primary and secondary school, both the Qu'ran and the *Green Book* were on the curriculum. All of them had also undergone military training since the age of 15.

However, what distinguished the civil from the military students was that the second group, unlike the first, belonged to a body with a hierarchical and rigid framework. The university students were enrolled in five different faculties, whereas if the student officers represented two years, they were part of the single and same institution where they shared daily life, met regularly, and heard doctrinal discourse more often than their university colleagues. As for the students of the WMA, although they were divided into different sections, they had the characteristic of belonging to an institution which claimed to be model and unique; right from when they joined they were selected for their understanding of the revolution and their motivations.

In principle we could therefore expect significantly different responses from each of the four groups considered. The women officers' group is a priori the most representative of Jamahiryan ideology.

2. THE OBSERVATION INSTRUMENT; THE QUESTIONNAIRE

The observation instrument[3] contained eight sections, each covering a series of conflictual situations. Some of these situations appeared in several sections of a written questionnaire submitted in Arabic to the members of the four groups sampled.

This questionnaire contained fourteen questions (I to XIV), each corresponding to a typical conflict situation. It in fact called for 19 separate answers, as one of the questions (XI) was subdivided into 6 sub-questions[4].

In the sections:

3 The English translation of the questionnaire text, in the order the questions were presented to the interviewees (I to XIV), is reproduced in the appendix.

4 Some questions covered several sections, which explains why the number of questions grouped by themes is more than the total of 19.

  - 7 questions related to husband/wife relationships (III, V, VI, VII, VIII, XI, XII);
  - 4 concerned parents/daughter relationships (I, II, IV, X);
  - 2 related to sharing the tasks at home (XI – containing 6 sub-questions, XII);
  - 5 were specifically devoted to the profession of female officer (I, III, IV, VI, X);
  - 4 concerned more a woman's job in civil life (V, VII, VIII, IX);
  - 4 concerned women holding military or civil jobs without distinction (XI, XII, XIII, XIV);
  - 3 concerned the notions of salary, budget and saving (II, IX, XI);
  - 1 related to the wearing of the veil and women's respectability (XI).

Problem of interpreting and classifying the answers

For different reasons, the answers obtained sometimes contained a degree of ambiguity.

We were not in a position to "test" this questionnaire by a prior study, as we did not fail to do in other situations. In composing it, we were therefore not able to fully outline the implications of certain imagined conflicts, nor discern certain differences in value attached to them, and even less anticipate the intellectual progress of the subjects questioned (as the answers given could in any circumstance only be the fruit of the experiences lived and the values respected).

Upon analysis, certain conflict situations appeared to have inadequate illustration. So, giving up saving (to satisfy an individual need – buying their own car – question II), giving up keeping their income to dispose of it freely (in the case of married women, who are allowed to do so by the Qu'ran – question IX), may signify on the part of working woman either obedience and submission to the environment, or adherence to the Jamahiryan concept of joint possessions and sharing, or again a liking for Western-style individualism. In other cases, the same answer may cover two opposed attitudes; so, the preference stated for marrying the cousin suggested by the parents rather than the colleague chosen according to the heart's inclination (question IV) may mean either giving up the personal wish, or the conviction that closeness of origin is an essential factor for understanding in the couple.

It is obvious that situations of commitment and duty connected with military environments (whether vocation, motivations for choosing the armed profession, reactions to the change of posting or a mobilisation order etc) employ concepts of work and responsibility which are substantially different from those prevailing in a university environment. Men or women civil students who on the whole did not have a very positive attitude to the military career, particularly as regards that of a woman officer, would naturally be less involved in the hierarchical questions (question III), whereas, the other way round, the call to take part in a medical or scientific congress (question VIII) would not be thought very motivating by soldiers, men or women).

Here we touch on the fact that a purely statistical analysis of pre-determined answers can be inadequate, even contain the risk of errors in interpretation. So it seemed essential to rely on the comments added to the answers[5], of which there were fortunately many, and sometimes to put together certain sections or categories of answers which, when together, could contribute significantly to understanding.

For the analysis and the significance of the results, we will make a distinction between the answers given, question by question, on the one hand by the students of the WMA regarded as reference sample (or standard), and on the other by the other three groups questioned (male student officers, female and male university students).

3. THE CHOICE OF THE WMA AS REFERENCE STANDARD

As indicated above, the measuring instrument did not have a normative value in itself, and so the answers obtained were in no way compared with a norm. It was only possible to record differences which were statistically significant, not

5 These comments were either written directly on the questionnaires, or verbal and received when the completed questionnaires were handed in.

precise and quantifiable differences in relation to a fixed element, norm or yardstick.

In Part II of this book we saw that the female student officers were selected right from their entry into the Academy according to their understanding of the revolution, that they were then systematically trained in conformity with the Jamahiryan values, and that in this way they were supposed to become a new model of woman, that of the "liberated woman". Their opinions can therefore be regarded as relatively representative of the new spirit.

So it seems justified for us to regard the WMA as the reference sample, or, if you like, the norm. The differences in opinion of the other three groups compared with those of the WMA student officers will therefore give us a more or less precise idea of the situation of the mentalities of the future élites, as well as of the road still to be gone along before the declared objective – a generalised change in mentalities – will be achieved.

Chapter II

Analysis of data collected

The following table reproduces all the answers given to the questionnaire, on the one hand by the 33 student officers of the WMA, and on the other by the 146 interviewees making up the other three groups (student officers at the MMA, male and female university students).

1. COMPARISON OF THE COHESION WITHIN THE FOUR GROUPS: INTRA-POSITIONAL CONSENSUS

From the start a certain cohesion of opinion appears within the four groups, producing quite a high degree of consensus in the ideas expressed. Here we are taking the term of "consensus" to mean a (more or less) large majority of opinion – that is, positively or negatively, 60% or more of the sample.

In our analysis we must make a distinction between the intra-positional consensus (that is the degree of agreement within the same group) and the inter-positional consensus (representing the degree of agreement between the members of different groups on the subject of a particular role.

QUESTIONS	ANSWERS (in %)		
(The complete text of each question is given in Appendix A)	of the WMA students	of the other three groups	
		MMA	F st.	M st.
I. 1. Give up the WMA	3%	33%	64%	58%
2. Enrol at the WMA nevertheless	97	67	36	42
II. 1. Give up saving for car	6	39	22	45
2. Save nevertheless	94	61	78	55
III. 1. Child with mother	21	33	62	50
2. Child with somebody else	33 }79	34} 67	10} 38	18} 50
3. Child with father	46	33}	28}	32}
IV. 1. Marry cousin (forced)	0			
2. Marry cousin (own choice)	48} 100	39	40	28
3. Marry military colleague	52}	61	60	72
V. 1. Give up work	0	30	18	36
2. Refuse to have more children	100	70	82	64
VI. 1. Children left with other people	24	22	16	30
2. With mother	0 100	30 70	30 60	40 60
3. Both parents in turn	70	48	44	30
VII. 1. Give up work	3	63	42	37
2. Neglect the housework	6	0	0	2
3. Leave children in nursery	91	37	58	61
VIII. 1. Go to the congress with the delegation	48	22	18	29
2. Not go to the congress	52	78	82	71
IX. 1. Give up the salary	24	31	6	30
2. Give up part of the salary	55	57	72	64
3. Keep it all for herself	21	12	22	6
X. 1. Terminate contract	0	43	65	68
2. Leave parents	100	57	35	32
XII. 1. Management by husband	0	7	2	24
2. Management by wife	0	0	0	0
3. Management by couple	100	93	98	76
XIII. 1. Husband on holiday alone: normal	0	0	6	8
2. Allowed sometimes	88	69	51	74
3. Unacceptable	12	31	43	18
XIV 1. Veil better	15	64	43	54
2. Not essential	85	36	57	46
XV. Husband participating in:	52	57	51	50
Cleaning house	33	31	14	30
Doing washing	52	69	65	56
Ironing	33	31	18	32
Preparing meals	85	86	75	62
Looking after children	100	93	100	90
Shopping				
– Husband participates in everything	33	31	20	28
– Husband participates in nothing (except shopping)	15	7	14	32

The intra-positional consensus tells us about the degree of internal cohesion of the groups. Depending on its level of intensity, we can come to a conclusion regarding the strength with which the roles (old or new) are imposed within each group. Its dispersion can be regarded as giving the scale of the degrees of intra-positional consensus.

The following four tables (A to D) reproduce the range of dispersion of the answers for each group. This is necessarily unequal depending on the questions and the samples.

What is immediately striking is the fact that the rate of consensus within the WMA sample is very high. This confirms the degree of cohesion of this group, a probable sign of its members' strong identification with the new models and new values. So the answers of the WMA group are by far the least dispersed, for 9 questions the reference consensus is even almost unanimous (95 to 100%).

Table A: Dispersion of WMA answers

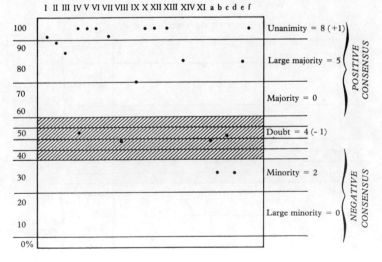

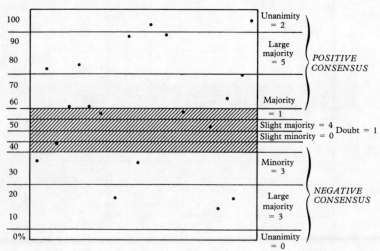

Table B: Dispersion of MMA answers

Table C: Dispersion of female university students' answers

Table D: Dispersion of male students' answers

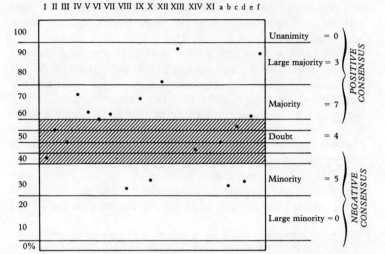

It does not reach the rate of the standard sample in any of the other three groups.

In the three other groups (Tables B, C and D), only that of the MMA students shows a relatively high consensus (positive and negative), going partially – although to a lesser degree – in the same direction as that of the women student officers, particularly with regard to "military situations". With a total intra-positional consensus of 16 (see Table E below), this group also demonstrates a high degree of cohesion.

As for the group of female university students, it demonstrates both quite a pronounced positive consensus (unanimity for 2 questions, large majority for 5 others) and a negative consensus for 6 questions (highest level of negative consensus among the four groups, which tends to express an apparent detachment from the Jamahiryan concepts and a certain proximity to the patriarchal values).

Finally, it appears that the group of male university

students is manifestly more hesitant in its judgements. The dispersion of the latter shows its weak cohesion (non-consensus on 7 questions, positive intra-positional consensus only reaching quite a low level).

Across the four groups, we note that several questions show a dispersion of opinions which is such that we cannot legitimately speak of intra-positional consensus for them (the votes show neither a clear majority nor minority). These questions were in general thought "difficult" or "ambiguous", which could mean that the non-consensus was due not the group's lack of cohesion, but to a semantic or conceptual stumbling-block.

The following table summarises the results of the analyses of intra-positional consensus by group:

From this schematic table we can repeat that for all the

TABLE E: *Intra-positional consensus showing the cohesion of the group by number of questions obtaining 60% or more acceptance or rejection*

	CONSENSUS			Non-consensus	Total number of questions
	Positive	Negative	Total		
WMA	14	2	16	3	19
MMA	11	5	16	3	19
F. students	9	5	14	5	19
M. students	8	4	12	7	19

groups, the consensus is overall positive, and therefore goes in the direction defined at the beginning as "modernist". However, the intra-positional consensus data does not allow us to conclude with certainty that the other three groups are really ideologically close to the reference sample.

So the need arises to analyse the inter-positional consensus, or degree of agreement between members of the different groups regarding the same role. This analysis is the subject of the following passages. We will give the content of the answers supplied question by question, trying to determine how the opinions obtained from the male and female interviewees express their judgement – positive or negative– in the context of the opposing ideologies, and in relation to them.

There remains a final analysis to be made; that of the relative influence of the background, defined as the father's level of education, on the "modernist" or "traditionalist" options of all those questioned.

2. INTER-POSITIONAL CONSENSUS

A. The marginal influence of the social background

The two following tables give a visual comparison of all the results of the study and allow the opinions obtained to be read directly overall.

The first table (F) shows the answers broken down by social origin, according to the three categories defined by the father's level of education. The second (G) presents the answers comparatively for each sample selected at the beginning (WMA, MMA, female university students and male university students).

Table F demonstrates firstly the slight difference of opinion revealed by comparing the judgements expressed according to the three categories – illiterate father, average level of education, or higher level. The distribution by social origin shows a clearly marked inter-positional consensus between the three categories. So, the factor "father's level of education" taken as an indicator of the social background only plays a part in the judgements made in two situations; the use of nurseries (question VII) and the wearing of the veil (XIV), two areas where the interviewees from illiterate backgrounds showed themselves to be more "traditionalist" than the others.

Furthermore, a study of Table F shows more clearly than Table G that there is a majority inter-positional consensus, positive or negative, for all the questions.

B. The differential impact of the ideology on the four groups

As Table G shows, the four samples present, in relation to each other, differences in opinion which are statistically very significant.

We are now going to try to situate, question by question, the average opinion of each of the groups, comparing firstly the answers supplied by the WMA student officers defined as the reference sample (section A), and then the answers – separate or together – of the other three groups; male student

TABLE F

	QUESTIONS
I	Enrol at the WMA
II	Save for a car
III	Give priority to profession (care of child)
IV	Choose freely, follow heart
V	Refuse to have more children
VI	Give priority to profession (entrust children to others)
VII	Give priority to profession (use nursery)
VIII	Take part in congress abroad
IX	Keep all or part of salary
X	Leave parents' house (to honour contract)
XII	Manage family budget together
XIII	Accept husband sometimes going on holiday alone
XIV	Make self respected without wearing veil
XI	a) Clean the house
	b) Do washing
	c) Do ironing
	d) Do cooking
	e) Look after children
	f) Do shopping

– – – – – Illiterate background
———— Average background
············· Diploma background

198

TABLE G

%	QUESTIONS
	I Enrol at the WMA
	II Save for a car
	III Give priority to profession (care of child)
	IV Choose freely, follow heart
	V Refuse to have more children
	VI Give priority to profession (entrust children to others)
	VII Give priority to profession (use nursery)
	VIII Take part in congress abroad
	IX Keep all or part of salary
	X Leave parents' house (to honour contract)
	XII Manage family budget together
	XIII Accept husband sometimes going on holiday alone
	XIV Make self respected without wearing veil
	XI a) Clean the house
	b) Do washing
	c) Do ironing
	d) Do cooking
	e) Look after children
	f) Do shopping

– – – – –   WMA student officers
———————   MMA student officers
·············   Female university students
———————   Male university students

199

officers, female university students and male university students (section B).

Question I: A girl wants to go to the Women's Military Academy, but her parents are totally opposed to this plan, and she has not managed to persuade them. What must she do?
1. She must give up the idea of enrolling.
2. She must enrol nevertheless, hoping that her parents will change their mind later."

A. By choosing the second answer almost unanimously (with one exception), the WMA students expressed first of all their strong motivation for a career which, beyond a professional choice, represents a deep commitment for them.

But their consensus also expresses an explicit reference to the Jamahiryan model; the "new" woman must take up her responsibilities and follow her personal vocation. If the applicant to the WMA in the question was not able to persuade her parents, we assume that it was rather a question of lack of trust in their daughter and respect for her convictions. In this case, the break with the family – which we can imagine would be inevitable – would in the end have been thought acceptable and allowed:

– "It's a question of her whole future, and also the future of the country, so she can't give in just like that".

– "Before, fathers had all the rights over their daughters, now that's finished".

– "If their arguments (the parents') aren't convincing, she has the right not to listen to them".

Certain comments made in the margin of the test show, however, that the female student officers expected that such a break would only be temporary (as was in fact the case for two students in the sample; cf. interviews in Part II, Chapter II):

– "Yes, she must enrol nevertheless. But she mustn't stop trying to persuade her family, the break must only be temporary".

B. As it is a conflict situation at the basis of a

military career, it is not surprising to find that the majority of the men student officers shared the same dominant opinion of their female colleagues (67% chose answer no. 2).

On the other hand, on the "civil" side, the majority of the male students (58%), like the female students (64%), thought that the girl wanting to go to the WMA should give up the idea of enrolling to conform to her parents' wishes.

Question II: "A girl wants to put the money that she earns away (in the bank) so as to be able to buy a car, which she needs for her work. Her parents do not agree, they say that they have to share everything, that she must give her money to the family, and that she can just as well take the bus to get about. What must she do?
1. She must give in to her parents and give up her savings account.
2. She must put her money away nevertheless".

A. As for the previous question, almost all the women student officers (94%) opted for the second answer, for them saving for a professional goal was justified, even if they had to go against their parents' wishes. It is to be noted, however, that the comments were not without some scruples:

– "She must put the money away, as it's for her work that she needs this car."

– "If the family needs her money, it's different, she can give them part of her salary, and put the rest in the bank."

– "It will still be necessary for her to explain things properly to her parents, to try and make them understand properly".

The choice made may be surprising in that the *Green Book* recommends sharing earnings and financial consensus for the family (where the Qu'ran, however, allows women full and complete disposal of their own income). So, in the eyes of these young single girls, the family consensus appears to be less of a priority than improving their personal working conditions. We will later see that the attitude would be different in the case of a married woman.

B. In the other groups, it was among the female (university students) that we found the highest percentage (78%) of opinions in favour of personal saving for a professional goal.

As for the two male groups, they move significantly away from the females' degree of consensus, while remaining in the majority in favour of the "modernist" solution (MMA 61%, students 55%).

Question III: "A young woman officer is given an important job on a military base. She is married and has three children. One of the children falls ill, he needs his parents. Should she stay with him and cancel her work? Should she ask her husband to stay with the child? Or should she look for another solution?
1. She must cancel her work and stay with the child.
2. She must go to work and entrust the child to somebody.
3. The father must look after the child on this occasion".

A. Almost 80% of the women student officers questioned gave priority to their role as soldiers over that of mothers, but stipulating that in this case the young woman officer who was victim of a conflict of roles must first of all try to get out of her work:
– "She should ask for permission to be absent from the barracks that day. If she doesn't get it, she will ask her husband to stay with their sick child".
– "The work is the most important thing, the father or the grandmother can replace her at home".
The father was the solution most often mentioned to take over. As most said, the sharing of responsibilities must be real:
– "The child doesn't only have a mother, the father has just as important a role. But if he too cannot get away, then they have to look for another solution, a friend or a neighbour".
We see that in the opinion of the women student officers, looking after a sick child was not thought to be a task exclusive to the mother.

B. A similar split characterises the attitude of the male student officers, 69% of whom gave priority to the military role of the woman officer who was also a mother.

But on the whole the "civil" students showed themselves to be more attached to her maternal function. 62% of the female students and 50% of the males in the "civil" groups expressed that they were in the majority in favour of women at home.

Question IV: "A young student officer wants to marry a military colleague, he understands her well and she is in love with him. Her parents are against this, as they want her to marry her cousin. She feels affection for her cousin with whom she gets on well, but she really loves her military colleague. What must she do?
1. She must obey her parents and marry her cousin.
2. She must follow her heart and marry the soldier."

A. This question received answers containing a certain ambiguity from the WMA students. This is because the option "marry the cousin", may mean either obeying the parents and submitting to traditions, or an option freely chosen on the basis of a reinterpretation of the same traditions. According to the comments, and in line with the statements obtained during the individual interviews (Part II, Chapter II), it is the second interpretation which must be selected here:
– "If there is mutual understanding, there is no reason at all for this woman officer to oppose her parents' wish".
– "There is no reason for opposing the marriage with the cousin because she gets on well with him".
– "As she likes her cousin, it's better for her to marry the one who is closer to her, as he is also close to her family".
– "If she hasn't been able to convince her parents of the value of her feeling for her boyfriend, she will have to marry her cousin, who for his part understands her well".

We notice the importance attached to mutual understanding and getting on, more essential for the couple's well-being than the love/passion aspect. On the other hand, all the student officers stipulated that there was no question at all of their marrying just any cousin against their own wish:

"It's because he understands her and they get on well that she must turn towards her cousin. Otherwise, it would be best for her to marry her military colleague, or not to get married yet".

In all cases, getting on well in the family was thought the most important factor. On the other hand, imposing her own candidate, especially if he was not accepted by the family, would not be suitable.

B. In the other three groups, a majority of roughly two-thirds (female students 60%, MMA 61%, male students 72%) opted for the love marriage.

It was on the whole among the men (students 28%, MMA 39%) that "marriage to the cousin" found less favour (compared with 48% at the WMA and 40% of the female university students).

Question V: "A married woman, mother of three children, likes her work. She does not want to have any more children, as she thinks she would no longer have the time to work. Her husband, however, would like a large family, six or seven children, and he wants her to leave work, as he thinks it is more useful (for a woman) to have children than to work in an office. What must she do?
1. She must give up her work to have more children.
2. She must carry on working and tell her husband she is not having any more children".

A. The group of WMA students was unanimous in its choice of Answer 2. So anyone who liked her work must be able to do it. The woman must not give in to the arguments and wishes of the husband, she is entitled to a certain personal fulfilment and must not become the slave neither of her husband nor of the children. Such is the opinion of the women officers:

1. "If they didn't have any children, it would be a different matter. But they already have three".

2. "The husband's arguments aren't valid, three children who are well brought up is much better than six or eight who are brought up by an ignorant mother".

One thing seems clear: as regards the students of the WMA, they had no intention at all of turning themselves into "breeding-hens"[1]. The women officers gave themselves the right to reject this role for themselves and intended to do what they wanted with their own bodies, within certain limits.

B. Of the female university students, only 18% would give up work and let the husbands impose their will, a strong majority therefore expressed themselves to be in favour of the woman's right to an independent professional life.

Among the men (soldiers and civilians together), one-third of the sample (30 and 36% respectively) wanted to force the women, in this particular case, to sacrifice her job so as to devote herself to producing a very large family. It seems that here the argument of "social usefulness" – in a severely under-populated country – concealed the expression of ordinary male sexism.

Question VI: "An officer couple, both captains, have four children. They work on a military base. War breaks out and they are each called to their respective units. What must they do?
1. Leave their children to other people.
2. Only the mother must stay with the children.
3. They must stay with their children in turn."

A. For the students of the WMA, in the event of war this soldier couple would find itself called to share their responsibilities both in the professional field and

1 Speaking before girls from a secondary school on the subject of marriage, Ghadafi declared: "What value does marriage have today? You prepare a diploma to in the end give yourselves to a nobody, who only sees in you a maid . . . If only 5% do not accept this situation for themselves! As for the 95%, they have every liberty to make what they want of themselves; maids, laundry-women, breeding-hens for 18 months before another breeding-hen takes their place".

on the family level. So no woman student officer intended her role as a mother to take precedence over that as soldier. The majority (76%) thought that it was up to both partners to take it in turns with their children and thus to share the parental role equally. A quarter of them would even be prepared to entrust the children to other people so as to give priority in all cases to the defence of their native country:

– "For the woman officer, it's just the consequence of her profession, of her commitment".

– "After all, other people can look after the children. What must take precedence above all is the general interest".

B. In each of the other three groups, roughly one-third of the interviewees thought that in the event of war the soldier wife should give priority to her maternal role.

This may be surprising a priori on the part of the MMA student officers, whose opinion was apparently the same as the civil interviewees' on this subject. Some comments, however, explain more about the way in which these future officers saw the role of the woman soldier:

– "The children are the most precious heritage for the country. The soldiers' duty is also to protect them".

– "Defending the children means at the same time defending the country".

The majority of the three groups (MMA 70%, female and male students 60%), however, shared the opinion of the reference sample, believing that fulfilment of her duty as an officer remained the priority for the woman soldier.

As for looking after the children in this exceptional situation, almost half (48%) of the MMA students and 44% of the female university students were of the opinion that both parents should share this responsibility, whereas the male university students would entrust this role to other people (30%) as much as to the two parents (30%).

206

Question VII: "A married woman, a mother, likes her work a lot. But, very tired by her double task at home and outside, she asks her husband, who is free every afternoon, to help her in her domestic chores. He refuses and says: You only have to stay at home and leave work. What must she do?
1. She must give up work.
2. She must carry on working and neglect the housework a little.
3. She must put her children in a nursery".

A. 91% of the young women soldiers thought that a mother must not give up all her time to the family. They thought it desirable for the woman to exist outside her maternal role, and that like the husband she also had a professional life:
– "The woman must not give in to her husband's selfish tendency".

If the latter refused to share the responsibilities and chores within the couple, the overwhelming majority would advise the mother in difficulty to turn to the new structures created (creches, nurseries), and only 6% would seek the solution in neglecting the housework[2].

For one only, there would be no other solution than to give in and resign.

B. In agreement with the reference sample, the male (63%) and female (58%) university students largely granted the woman the right to independent work and recommended the use of crèches and nurseries:
– "There is no reason for her to sacrifice herself completely to the housework because her husband is selfish" (female student).
– "She must carry on working on condition that the children do not become victims of the father's selfishness" (male student).

On the other hand, a majority of men student officers (63%) recommended that the married woman

2 This demolishes the opinion of their male colleagues, many of whom thought that the students of the WMA would in general make not such good housekeepers as the other women. See Part II, Chapter III.

gave up her professional role for the benefit of the children:
– "It's better for her to keep her health and not get irritated with the children".
– "Her work isn't all that important. It isn't a military commitment. The best thing is for her to resign".

Her presence in a civil job is therefore thought to be of less use to society. As they do not grant a married woman's professional work priority, the men soldiers were also clearly less favourable to the "crèche" solution. In this, moreover, they adopt an attitude more in line with Jamahiryan doctrine, as the *Green Book* tends to criticise the institution of crèches and nurseries (at least for regular use).

Question VIII: "The husband is in agreement that his wife, a doctor, exercises her profession. One day she has to go to a congress abroad in a delegation with colleagues for one week. Her husband does not want her to go, in fact he is jealous that she is going with other men that he does not know. What must she do?
1. She must go with the delegation all the same, if she has obtained an exit permit.
2. She must give up the idea of going to the congress".

A. As regards the women student officers, opinions here were completely divided. There were in particular just as many who thought that the woman doctor should give up the idea of taking part in the congress abroad (52%) as who thought that the wife should not consider her husband's feelings nor resign herself to putting up with his jealousy and authority (48%).

Those who advocated giving up the idea from the beginning justified this opinion either by the importance of good relations between the couple (for them the stake did not seem high enough to justify threatening the peace of the household), or by the strong doubt as to the morality of the doctor wife (who hadn't obtained her husband's trust):

– "Perhaps she doesn't deserve his trust"
– "She isn't really a liberated woman (in the Jamahiryan sense) if she doesn't know her own limits".
– "If her husband is jealous, it's certain that he has his reasons".

So, curiously, the female interviewees identified more with the husband's motivations than those of the wife (who, in this case, was not a soldier). And in so far as the emphasis was put first on mutual understanding and agreement within the couple, the comments show that it was rather up to the woman to make an effort and to show herself to be worthy of the man's trust.

B. In the other three groups, we found that the majority of women as well as men (female students 82%, MMA 78%, male students 71%) thought that the husband's jealousy was "acceptable", or, at the very least, that it constituted a factor which it was normal to take into account. The "old reflexes" here seemed to play a full role. The comments gave a good illustration of the reasons for giving up the idea, which in their view was necessary:
– "This congress isn't a professional necessity".
– "The event isn't worth a marital conflict".

In these three groups, as in the reference sample, they too did not deny the necessity for understanding and mutual trust within the couple. But the majority thought that it was up to the woman to generate this trust, and it was up to her to convince her husband. In any case, if this plan was going to create conflict, she should give it up. In other words, the interest and the harmony of the couple took precedence over personal fulfilment or individual pleasure.

The husband's jealousy was not regarded *a priori* as an anomaly, nor as an "illness". Giving up the idea of going on the trip and taking part in the congress was not because it was the woman's duty to obey the husband; this obligation was necessary because of the concern to maintain good relations at home.

Question IX: "The husband earns a good salary, his wife, who works, also earns money. She intends to keep her salary for herself, as the household does not need it at all. The husband refuses, wanting them to share everything. What must she do?
1. She must give her salary up to her husband and the family.
2. She must give her husband at least part of her salary.
3. She must keep all her salary for herself".

A. The opinions expressed here by the WMA students' appeared to vary substantially; although 55% of them would agree to giving up part of their salary for the household, 24% would agree to sharing all of it, whereas 21% intended to keep it all for themselves.

It is true that the situation presented is not itself without ambiguity. In a way there is the husband defending the principle of the *Green Book* according to which sharing earnings must be the norm, whereas the Qu'ran allows women to keep their own income, the husband being obliged to maintain the family.

How, then, must we interpret the range of answers? The comments do not help a lot, and analysis remains difficult. What the answers of the WMA students do show is that they often hesitated between the "patriarchal" opinion of submission ("give up everything"), but which also means "share everything" in the family, according to the precepts of the *Green Book*, and a "modernist" attitude, consisting of keeping part of her salary for herself as a guarantee of financial independence (preservation of a newly acquired freedom) and to sacrifice to a certain realism (to meet her own needs in the context of her work). A number of them, however, stated that the opinion consisting of giving up part of their salary (55%) or even all of it (24%) was not because of the marital requirement, but because they were in principle in agreement with the option of sharing.

B. More clearly than in the sample, in the other three groups the opinion prevails that it is normal for the woman to give up part of her salary to the family community (MMA 57%, male students 64%, female students 72%).

But whereas one-third of the men (MMA 31%, male students 30%) thought that the woman should not keep anything for herself, the female students showed themselves less inclined to share (6% would agree to "give it all up", 22% thought they would "keep it all").

Question X: "A woman officer lives with her parents while carrying out her functions at the barracks. One day, she is posted to another town, far from her parents, and she is forced to take accommodation there. Her parents do not want her to live alone, they want her to resign from the army. What must she do?
1. She must terminate her contract with the army and resign.
2. She must accept her new posting and leave the paternal home, as her own career is at stake".

A. 97% of the WMA students questioned replied that the woman officer did not have the right to resign through sentimentality (to please her parents, her neighbours etc) and that she should be above the "What will they say?" All agreed that in this case she should leave the parental home, either at the cost of a compromise (6%), and even if it were to go as far as breaking off from her parents. It thus seems that in their view the traditional obligation for a young unmarried woman to live with her parents is obsolete:
– "She is an adult, she knows how to defend herself alone, she must rely on herself. The rest, the traditional ideas, the fear of criticism from others, they mustn't govern her conduct".

Some of them, however, (6%), tried to avoid the break, the family conflict. They suggested negotiating with the military authorities (a solution not given in the test questionnaire):
– "She must first go and discuss it with her superiors. But, if there is an emergency, she must accept her change."

B. The opinion of the group of MMA students shows quite a large consensus around the concept of

211

the "military obligation". 57% of them thought that it was the woman officer's duty to obey and to leave the parental home. The remaining 43% suggested in their attitude an explanation inspired by the very poor regard in which they held the career of the woman soldier.

– "Resigning is not a very serious loss, the army will work quite well without her".

As for the two university groups, they agreed in a consensus the other way round; 68% of the males and 65% of the females argued for resignation in observance of the customs and in favour of maintaining cohesion with the family group. Only one-third of the civil students thus took into consideration the "pursuit of the personal career" aspect of the woman officer.

Question XI: "By whom must the family budget be managed?
1. By the husband alone.
2. By the wife alone.
3. By the couple together".

A. The students of the WMA unanimously opted for management of the family budget together. They thought that husband and wife should share the responsibility of the expenses and total management of the budget. This, however, was not at all normal practice in traditional Libya, where, except in the limited case of widowhood (the wife then sometimes managing her budget) only the husband was called on to know the resources and the expenses of the home. In this respect, the unanimous choice of the women soldiers goes completely in the innovative direction of the *Green Book*.

B. An almost identical degree of consensus characterises the opinion of two other groups; 97.5% of the female university students and 93% of the MMA students also thought that the family budget should be managed by both partners together.

As for the group of male university students, it was substantially different from the previous ones; a quarter of the sample would like the budget to be managed by the husband alone.

Question XII: "Is it normal for the husband to go on holiday on his own, leaving his wife and children at home?
1. Yes, that is normal and acceptable.
2. Yes, but it must not happen too often.
3. No, it is not acceptable".

A. None of the WMA students would agree to their husbands going on holiday and leaving wife and children at home. However, very many (88%) thought that there would be nothing to complain about if it only happened "now and again". Several added that in this case they would also reserve the right to sometimes go away on their own. In this area, the husband could not accord himself unilateral privileges or liberties, they had to share leisure as well as the other things, by accepting a certain mutual independence.

A minority (12%) thought that the husband going on holiday alone was unacceptable. But on this point, as for any other, the interviewees stressed the opportunity of mutual concessions to help maintain good relations, and the need to observe strict equality between husband and wife.

B. The majority in the other three groups also thought, all in all, that it was normal for the husband to sometimes go on holiday alone, but on condition that it remained an exception (male university students 74%, MMA students 69%, female university students 51%).

The female university students appeared the least conciliatory in this matter (43% thought that it was unacceptable for the husband to go away without taking his family), while almost a third of the male student officers expressed the same opinion.

Question XIII: "In your opinion is a woman who goes out in public with her hair carefully covered to be thought more respectable than one who goes out with her hair free, even though correctly dressed?

213

1. Yes, it is preferable for a woman to cover her head in public, she will be respected more.
2. No, she can make herself be respected just as well without that, dress is not really important".

A. As the free statements noted during the individual interviews with the women officers led us to believe, the great majority of them (85%) subscribed to the view that a woman no longer had to be veiled in order to be respected, and that neither the veil nor the tchador could now be regarded as synonymous with faith and belief.

A minority (15%), however, thought that in the present state of Libyan society "which is not yet completely liberated", it was preferable for women to cover their heads in public. But was it conviction or comfort and convenience? It was better for them to put a scarf over their hair as then they would be more at peace.

B. As for the other groups, it seems that a majority of the men (64% of the MMA students, 54% of the university students) thought that it was better for women to go out in public with their heads covered.

But there was a notable difference between the opinion of the men students, more traditionalist, and that of the female students, 57% of whom thought that wearing the veil was no longer important and that they could just as well be respected without this sign of attachment to tradition (or, for others, to religion).

Question XIV: "In your opinion is it normal that in a marriage with children, where both husband and wife work, the husband must help his wife:

To clean the house?	Yes/No
To do the washing?	Yes/No
To do the ironing?	Yes/No
To prepare the meals?	Yes/No
To look after the children?	Yes/No
To do the shopping?	Yes/No".

A. Overall, one-third of the reference sample (WMA students) thought it normal for the husband to help with all the chores at home.

Two-thirds, on the other hand, showed themselves to be more selective. Although there was unanimity as regards the husband participating in the shopping (which we will remember was traditionally done by the master of the house), and a large majority (85%) thought that the husband should do his share of looking after and bringing up the children, opinions were divided regarding his participation in the ironing (52%) and cleaning the house (48%). As for the cooking and the washing, two-thirds of the sample thought that these activities traditionally reserved for women must remain a female function. Some student officers explained their choice as follows:

– "The husband mustn't get involved in everything. Dirty washing isn't a man's job. For the cooking, the wife has her habits".

– "I think it is better for the woman to keep herself an area where she can organise herself as she wants. And for the rest, they can share everything".

We note here, as for Question IX (keeping part of her salary for herself), that the student officers showed a tendency to want to keep a kind of personal or financial independence.

B. If we consider the answers supplied by the other three groups overall, we find that a large majority of the interviewees – men and women – thought it natural for the husband to take part in at least some of the activities at home, and they were therefore in agreement with the opinion of the reference sample. But the answers varied quite substantially depending on the nature of the different domestic tasks – as was also the case in the reference sample:

– "Looking after the children and doing the shopping in town were regarded by the great majority as "mixed" tasks.

– The votes were much more divided for cleaning the house.

– Finally, on the question of preparing the meals or doing the washing, a distinct group said they were against the possible participation of men.

By comparing the answers of one group to the other, a significant difference appears between the opinion of the soldiers and that of the civilians; the former showed themselves to be more positive towards the husband's extended participation in the various tasks (one-third would take part in everything, compared with a quarter of the civilians). In addition, the majority (almost 70%) would be inclined to take over the ironing.

On the whole, in women we found a greater reserve towards the husband taking part in the household chores, which shows on their part either a stronger attachment to the traditional female roles, or a desire to keep a particular autonomous area, or both reasons at the same time.

Chapter III

Interpretation of data
and evaluation of results

1. *THE GREEN BOOK* AND THE REFERENCE SAMPLE: THE CONCORDANCE OF OPINIONS

Following this systematic analysis, the opinions of the WMA students defined as the reference sample can overall be summarised by the statement that they largely correspond to the ideological options of the *Green Book*, illustrated and complemented by Ghadafi's speeches. These options, which have become articles of faith for the women officers, can be expressed essentially as follows:

– a woman's right to work and personal fulfilment;
– the right to self-affirmation, in opposition to the parents, even disobeying them in certain cases;
– the right to freely choose their future husband, within the limits of family approval;
– the right to limit the size of the family, in the mother's interest and in order to improve the quality of inter-family relations;
– the sharing of responsibilities by the couple and the family, in particular with regard to the children;

– the necessity for mutual agreement and understanding between the partners;

– the obligation to make some individual concessions, when it concerns the well-being of the couple and the family as a unit.

However, contradictorily, there are two trends which diverge from this doctrinal line:

– firstly, the inclination of most of the young women soldiers to want not to give up certain areas or competences traditionally reserved for women (doing the cooking, the washing etc) and which, according to the new concepts, could just as well be shared with the husband;

– secondly, the tendency already mentioned to give priority to the military profession over family and maternal obligations, going so far as to prefer to adopt a solution such as the day-nursery (which was in no way encouraged in the *Green Book*).

This over-evaluation of the profession, characteristic of the opinion of the young women who had opted for the army as a career, may be explained by its being rooted in a real vocation. It expresses the role of "model" which they are supposed to have to play. It also seems to demonstrate a certain tendency to individualism, an individualism of which it is difficult to say whether it constitutes a personality trait associated with the profile of the woman officer, or whether it appears as a reaction and defence against the constrictive practices of life in the barracks.

2. REFERENCE SAMPLE AND OTHER GROUPS: SIMILARITIES AND DIFFERENCES

Comparison of the opinions of the WMA sample with those of the other three groups shows firstly that the quasi-unanimity of opinion in the reference sample was hardly ever matched in the other three groups (except in 3 situations out of 19).

However, on several points the ideas of the latter were the same as those of the reference. So, for 11 questions out of 19, the majority of the three groups opted for answers defined at the start as moving in the direction of the "modern" values. This majority apparently seems to agree

on a certain number of principles, still relatively new in Libyan society, such as:
- a woman's right to work, not only for economic reasons, but also for personal fulfilment;
- a woman's right to a certain independence, which is symbolised by having her own car;
- the right, within certain limits, to dispose of her own body (rejection of the role of "breeding-machine");
- the right to take an equal part with the man in managing the family budget (and therefore in decisions or taking responsibilities in a non-traditional area);
- the reciprocity of obligations by the couple (sacrifice of personal interest to collective interest);
- condemnation of traditional male selfishness;
- recognition of a social role and obligations as a citizen for women as well as men;
- agreement on sharing certain tasks (and not sharing others) in the home.

By cross-checking the answers and making a qualitative analysis of the comments, we find that despite these similarities, some differences appear in the interpretation of the situations, to varying degrees in the three groups.

It was the group of soldiers from the MMA which came closest qualitatively and quantitatively to the reference sample. This confirms the importance of the influence of the ideological discourse, as the student officers, men and women, are exposed to it more than the civilians. The agreement of opinions between male and female soldiers is shown firstly in all the situations relating to the armed profession and the responsibilities arising therefrom. So for the large majority of men officers, it seems normal for a woman officer to sacrifice the parental link to her vocation, which on the other hand is not accepted by the majority of civilians. In the same way, the majority of the male student officers, like their female colleagues, thought that the career and not breaking the military contract were priorities, even at the risk of conflict with the parents, and regardless of "What they will say".

Outside the military area, they, like their colleagues from the WMA, defended the need to share responsibilities within the couple, particularly towards the children and including looking after them. In only one situation did we find that the opinion of the men officers not only diverged from that of the civilian groups, but was in contrast to the female officers' judgements; this was on the institution of the nursery, literally rejected by the male soldiers, for whom priority in this case was the maternal, and not the professional, role. By this option, they showed, however, that they were closer to the line drawn in the *Green Book*, and more respectful of its precepts than the reference sample itself. This confirms an over-evaluation of their professional role by the WMA students, who without too many scruples favoured recourse to the nursery, giving priority to the exercise of their profession.

On this subject it is interesting to compare these results with those of a brief survey, using the same questionnaire, carried out among a limited group of members of a Women's Revolutionary Committee (consisting of seven young women); their answers precisely match those of the majority of the women officers. There was one single exception, which concerned the opinion expressed on the subject of the conflict of roles; without exception the "revolutionary women" gave priority to the maternal role over the professional role, a result which again confirms the hypothesis of over-evaluation of their role by the women at arms.

As we have just seen for the soldiers, the opinions expressed do not always hold the same significance; sometimes they need to be deciphered according to the context or the significance attached to conflict situations which are not necessarily seen in the same way. In certain cases it seems necessary to make a distinction between real consensus and apparent consensus, or pseudo-consensus.

In any case, it seems necessary to make this distinction for the answers supplied by the group of female university students. Do their judgements fundamentally refer to one and the same ideology? At least a fraction of the female students seemed to have the same opinion as the reference sample, but in a slightly different spirit; that of a feminist demand based on a certain modernism, while at the same time revealing itself to be also attached to a number of traditional values. In these women we therefore see, as a sort of self-defence behaviour, the affirmation of an individualism expressed by the desire to keep a private area in "modernity" for themselves (the right to work, keep the salary for themselves, have their own car), as well as in the traditional female areas (bringing up and looking after children, mother's prerogatives).

To what should we attribute the female students' attachment to certain traditions in particular? Is it fundamentally the perpetuation of the female image represented by the mother? Or a simple lack of confidence in themselves, apprehension about being distanced from custom? Or is it the fear of loss of independence – the little which they have in fact – the husband encroaching on their area (kitchen and motherhood as a means of exercising pressure and power), and distrust of a partner who is suspected of wanting to take over their "last bastion", indeed of exploiting new skills that his wife may have acquired for his own benefit? We found that for this reason some women refused to learn to drive, while demanding to learn other techniques likely to give them new areas of independence.

The comments and statements collected from the female students show that it is rather the second attitude which is more prevalent. They would therefore claim traditional women's roles to protect themselves more, without failing to demand their rights in the new areas. So these women appear as both ramparts of old traditions and as the driving-force of a new dynamism, Jamahiryan or "feminist". At this stage, we see that it is still hazardous to decide on the deep motives.

As for the group of male university students, it appears to be the most traditionalist of the three groups. When the majority goes in the same direction as the reference sample, in their case it is generally less pronounced. On several questions, the answers supplied in this group are dispersed, and no real majority opinion emerges.

In all cases, the male students appeared quite strongly attached to their prerogatives (taking their holidays as single men, doing the household shopping). But, more than all the other groups, the large majority rejected a forced marriage to a cousin, and opted in favour of the answer: "follow the inclination of one's heart". In this area they therefore

221

thought they were just as much the victims of the patriarchal laws as their sisters.

3. SHIFT FROM VERTICAL RELATIONS TOWARDS HORIZONTAL RELATIONS

We should return for a moment to the recapitulation of the questions as presented in Chapter I of this third part of the book, and compare the answers collected based on the distinction operating between situations relating on the one hand to daughter-parent relationships, and on the other those concerning relations between husband and wife.

It appears significant that in all cases affecting the relationship between two generations, an opposition which may go as far as a break-up is accepted without ambiguity by the majority of the interviewees, men and women, in all the groups.

On the other hand, as regards the life of the couple, the opinions obtained held many more subtle variations. The answers stressed the importance of maintaining communication and good relations by accepting mutual concessions; on this subject there was no difference of opinion between men and women, apart from a relative tendency on the part of the women to "understand" the husband's point of view more than the other way round[1].

From these observations, we are inclined to conclude that the majority of the interviewees rejected vertical authoritarian links (father – daughter), and favoured horizontal links of unity (dialogue and mutual understanding between husband and wife). Without breaking off all the family relations, the couple was now seeking a minimum autonomy (the option "marry the cousin" is ambiguous in this respect). As for the couple's internal relationship, it tends towards a reciprocal affectionate friendship which will no longer be the possible product of marriage, but must exist at the start and be the basis of life together.

Above we have emphasised the extreme importance of an

---

1 This can partly be explained by the difference in upbringing received in the family. The women's stronger identification to the situations presented in the questionnaire could also have influenced the results.

agreement on references by both sexes, an agreement believed to be essential for harmonious adjustment of the male and female roles. In this respect we noted that there was little difference between male and female opinions in the attitudes, whether positive or negative, towards the new values. There was only one exception to this observation; the attitude towards the veil. The men, both soldiers and civilians, were in agreement on this subject in an attitude which can be described as "traditionalist", in favour of the Islamic veil, whereas the majority of women declared they were in favour of rejecting this traditional "protection".

While conducting the survey, we sometimes found that girls who in the questionnaire declared they were against the wearing of the veil themselves wore it. This was the case of students whose parents forced them to wear the veil, otherwise they were not allowed to go out. In such a case the veil had become a "guarantee" and a "concession"[2]. Other students, veiled in the Iranian fashion, confessed no more or less than that they were following "a fashion" which had started at the university a short time ago.

As for Ghadafi, he has always declared that he is against the wearing of the veil. He has defined it in turn as a "trick", a "thing against nature", or again the "sign of a bourgeois mentality". It should be pointed out here that bedouin society does not have the woman's veil, and the veil is largely a heritage of urban bourgeois civilisation. So women from the country who go to live in town wear the veil to conform, not from a new religious conviction.

In our survey, the men questioned, civilians and soldiers, did not think in the same way as the Leader of the Revolution. The majority thought that it was still too early to remove this "protection" from women: "As long as male society is not liberated in the Jamahiryan sense, it is better for women to be protected from those who only see them as objects to be desired". Only a minority of men and women referred in this case to a religious obligation. Through the groups studied and at the intersection of the vertical and the

2 Cf. D. Abrous: "The veil signifies a rift from confinement. It conveys a particular way of questioning the separation between domestic space and public space. Wearing the veil is a kind of guarantee to be paid to transgress the wall erected between the inside and the outside", *Op. cit.*

horizontal, the dress custom thus seems to be more like a social interest than an article of dogma; each person is supposed to be free to decide whether to wear the veil and the traditional costume, female or male.

Here we will mention a characteristic of the behaviour of the Leader of the Revolution, whose extravagance and exuberance in dress have been remarked on so often, putting him poles apart from the sobriety of his daily life. This behaviour, which his opponents interpret as a sign of narcissism and capriciousness, does not only reflect an immoderate taste for appearance and theatre, it also denotes a concern to reinforce the verbal message, in a given situation and for a given audience, by the choice of a suitable image.

In Chapter 5 we noted the ability demonstrated by Ghadafi, each time he thought it necessary, to be an innovator: "The innovator, it is true, must first of all attract attention to himself". Consequently, in the non-conformism of his choices of clothing, we can see a deliberate attempt, whether successful or not each time, to effectively represent the image-symbol which he wants others to attribute to him in a given situation.

After completing the analysis of the data and the interpretation of the survey results, the subject of this Part III, it is appropriate to assess the impact of the *Green Book* ideology on the generation of the country's future civil and military élites.

At the start, we had wondered about the value of the three following hypotheses to the composition of our questionnaire, that is:

– the existence of a minimum consensus within the four groups in the sample in the direction of the new values;

– the observation of significant differences between these groups associated with their cohesion and their degree of exposure to the ideology;

– the influence of the father's level of education on the young people's adoption or rejection of the ideological concepts of the *Green Book*.

Of these three hypotheses, the first two were confirmed, the third not at all.

Through the existence of an almost general consensus, the results of the survey do show that a change in references is indeed taking place in the supposed direction, that is away from the patriarchal values. However, it is difficult to determine if the "modernist" ideological influence which we find exists is exclusively that of the *Green Book*, or if a certain imported feminism, less specifically Jamahiryan in character, does not act in parallel.

Likewise, we noted the existence of statistically significant differences between the four samples depending on the degree of ideological influence to which they were subjected. The opinions collected from the student officers of the MMA, which are closest to the Jamahiryan values incarnated by the reference sample (WMA), perfectly illustrate the validity of this hypothesis.

On the other hand, the hypothesis of an influence of social background (defined by the father's level of education) on adherence to the ideology, positively or negatively, was not confirmed.

These analyses, the remainder being somewhat speculative, do not permit clear conclusions, definitive ones even less so, on the development of mentalities in the young generation.

The observations made do indeed confirm that things are moving, that certain forces have been released, and that the movement is in a direction that we are tempted to define as "Jamahiryan feminism", in any case distinct from what is currently a Western feminist[3]. If we want to characterise what principally distinguishes the former from the latter, we would attribute to the "Jamahiryan feminism" a certain collective nature, as well as limits originating from an essentially Islamic attitude of community. As we have seen, the collective interest – whether the family community or another wider body – was regarded by the majority of the interviewees as having priority over the interest of the

---

3 This observation, although largely plausible, must be relativised. It would be necessary to carry out comparable surveys on different samples (from other comparable social backgrounds, other areas, even other countries).

individual; an individual who was acknowledged no real social existence outside the family, who could only live and survive as an integral part of the organic institution of the family cell[4].

So, fulfilment and liberation of the individual can only take place in harmony with the family, which in its turn must be the exact reflection of a Jamahiryan society claiming to be egalitarian and democratic. The fact that the collective interest (of the couple or the family) is recognised as a priority by the majority of the interviewees is clearly shown by the survey results, fully justifying this conclusion that the family organism must be amended, rebalanced, liberated ("decolonised", as Ghadafi says) as a priority, and that, for this purpose, and for this purpose only, the individual has the right to oppose, to revolt, and to refuse.

But the boundaries imposed on individualism – in other words on the rights granted to the individual, whether man or woman – are not rigidly defined. The collective interest and the individual interest can certainly co-exist, indeed coincide, in the absence of permanent conflict their limits remain negotiable, as are the roles and distribution thereof among the members of the family. However, for such negotiations to take place without too much conflict, it is important that both can refer to the same models and the same values. This leads to the unavoidable necessity for the emergence of "norms" called on to take the place of the laws of the patriarchate, and like them likely to have a universal value.

For as long as this is not the case, the search for a new equilibrium will produce adventure, or, if you like, acrobatics, particularly in the cases of relations between generations; the father, the first target and the first loser in the game of development of inter-family relations, will also logically be the first opponent. In Libya, it has only been possible to partially temper the generation conflict by the perpetual nature of this "respect for the old and the elders", so widely imparted to the young in the name of the family institution itself.

This is a conflict of generations, and not a conflict of

4 Cf. Part III of the *Green Book*.

sexes or social classes. If the father's level of education was shown to be without correlation to the children's adherence to the Jamahiryan values, the "democratic and open" spirit of certain families – from which, for example, most of the WMA students came – appears, however, to be an important, even determining factor, in the spread of "modernism". Where a certain ideological concordance and harmony of views has been found between the family environment, the school environment and their social environment, the probability of real resistance to change would be slight. *Vice versa*, a strict patriarchal background makes a multiplication of the conflict situations more than probable.

In this context, it would have been interesting to have had more data available on the families from which the interviewees came. In any case, the hypothesis according to which a strong positive correlation exists between "spirit of openness" in the background and the young people's adherence to the new values still has to be confirmed.

Here lies the whole difference between the change in mentalities to be introduced into a first generation (still brought up according to the patriarchal model) and the chances of change in a second (already influenced by the revolution). In this respect our sample is not homogenous; some of the interviewees already represented the second generation. Although the *Green Book* only appeared ten years or so after the start of the revolution, the ideas and the options that it expresses were being worked on, at least in their broad outlines, and were already launched by the revolutionary discourse. And now the followers and militants of this first period today form part of the generation of parents. For our male and female interviewees they already figure as precursors of the generation of "mutants".

In this study of the eradication of the old patriarchal concepts, we have only been able to collect an initial and inadequate output of information – the results of roughly ten years of efforts at conscious and organised ideological re-education. Our observations help to outline the development of mentalities of a whole generation and elaborates elements for problematics of social change in Libya.

Conclusions

Ghadafi and Jamahiryan Feminism

By constantly seeking to reconcile progress with a certain loyalty to traditions, Jamahiryan Libya is aiming to create its own model of society. The process of liberation for Libyan women, promoted to the rank of the revolution's "number one ally", comes under this heading of overall transformation. Is this, on the part of Colonel Ghadafi, purely and simply a tactical calculation, dictated either by the political interest represented by the "clientele" of women for the advent of direct democracy or for setting up the people in arms, or by the economic necessity of an under-populated country? Or does the option of the "woman at arms" as a model and symbolic image of the advancement of women stem from deeper sources?

It is always extremely hazardous to turn to elements of personal history linking behaviour in maturity to events from childhood. Nevertheless, we can try to explain the political leader's motives by relating them to the genesis of his social representations.

Almost nothing is known about the childhood of Moammar el Ghadafi, except a few main points; an initial happy and protected childhood, in an environment where the female element dominated (for him) – a mother with a strong personality, aunts, several sisters; the break away from this environment (around the age of nine) to go to school, a school which was rapidly going to put the child of the tribe in a position to go beyond his father's level of education, to show him as an intellectual in his background, to put him on a pedestal; a difficult integration into the new environment, provoking hostile feelings and self-defence reflexes, also probably loneliness and nostalgia (for nature, the desert, the maternal and tribal environment); an oppositional voluntarism with a tendency for reprisals sometimes difficult to control, and all in all a strong incitement for control of oneself, the effort of analysis, and an exaltation of the collective force provided by unity (groups of equals).

The *Green Book*, stressing the rights of the mother, may find one of its main sources in the child Moammar's particular experience of tribal life. It was at this stage that maternity was interiorised as a positive symbol. The rift associated with advancement by education would only accentuate this positive role of the mother, a source of life and change, compared with a relative effacement of the paternal image, associated with a tradition which was experienced as out of date. However, this man who as an adult is exceptional, nourished major complexes in childhood. For Ghadafi, the sun – a paternal symbol – by strong sublimation sometimes also becomes a symbol of love encompassing all, an essential symbol, as he himself sometimes declares. And yet we should distinguish the two contradictory trends that this sun symbol mobilises: a creator of life, thus giving all its power to the female principle; an agent of victory over the destructive fire which threatens humanity, and he thus allies himself with the national heroes.

The revolt against the father's power, and the aspiration to independence which increases strength tenfold and ignores boundaries (the space-time of the bedouin), are expressed with great intensity by Ghadafi. The revolutionary spirit, the taste for universalism, are nourished there, as is, on a higher level, religion as a return to the sources.

Can we go so far as to interpret the desire to recreate Libyan society as a quest for the original "djema'a", the tribal assembly, the basic democracy which enveloped his childhood? From the almost heretical concept of a new male-female relationship to women's total participation in social and political life, emerges an effort by the individual to rise above his surroundings, to put himself at the centre of the world, to make himself in turn dispenser of justice and creator, by sublimation of the narcissism of the child and by veneration of the mother. So, "Ghadafian feminism" can be understood first as a personal invention, poles apart from the dominant external influences such as the neighbouring contemporary feminist movements. So the symbol of "the woman at arms" doubtless goes back more to the image of Moammar el Ghadafi's own mother, who, it is said, was the best bow-woman in her tribe.

Nevertheless, it is obvious that if Ghadafi's personal experience had not encountered conditions suitable for implanting ideas which were so revolutionary compared with the background from which he came, his fantasies and his goals for change would never have managed to overcome Libyan society's first lines of resistance.

Paradoxically, according to the new model, women will be armed by men, by the Father, which is both the weak and the strong point of this particular liberation of Libyan women. It is a gift given by men, a gift granted and controlled from on high, and not the outcome of a struggle initiated by women themselves. In this respect, we must stress that although Ghadafi took great care to revive the female currents organised or in process of being so before the revolution, and a certain spontaneous feminism of the last (?) generation of mothers to be victims of the patriarchate, he has not always had the following of the people and the active support expected. It is obvious that in the eighties the Union of Libyan Women did not acquire the combative character which characterised the Western feminist movements during the preceding decades. Largely politicised, the Ittihad seems particularly like an instrument at the service of the socio-political programme in the Jamahirya.

There are not only negative sides to this situation logic. For the men, it spares them from a war of the sexes and a lot of feminist aggressivity towards them. Furthermore, the pressure of "Ghadafian feminism" is exercised as much, if not more, on men as on women. In this Ghadafi shows that he, like the new European feminists, has understood that the struggle of women alone is not enough to achieve the expected result, that it is necessary to dismantle the patriarchal system and promote a new order in men-women relationships.

It is also logical to try to use the *Green Book* and the "third universal theory" as a new set of references designed to help the young generation re-situate itself. The object is also to create a new family where, as soon as the child is born, he can find a referent of both sexes, both support for his identification and assurance against the automatic pre-eminence of one parent only. This is why Ghadafi attaches importance to the redefinition of roles; a fundamental interest in the new equilibrium to be created by an "equality within difference"[1]

We must acknowledge, however, that in Libya not everything is moving for the best of feminisms. We have stated our criticisms regarding an over-evaluation of their professional role by the student officers at the Women's Military Academy; it is as if the emergence of the individual was automatically bringing conflict caused by personal ambition opposed to the collective obligations; it is as if the slide towards Western-style individualism was the quasi-sanction of progress towards modernity.

As for the rest, if Utopia can shift things about, nothing guarantees that the effect will last. Cultural practices determined by on high must be interiorised and become the collective will or they will fade away. Overall, the advancement of Libyan women can only be completed by the initiative and continued effort of the interested parties themselves – and not without the men too feeling involved. This is one limit to the Leader's power.

There is nothing which lets us say that Libyan men, somewhat rebellious in character, but who have demonstrated their spirit of openness and a certain liking for innovation, assimilating many disturbing ideas such as the militarisation of women, cannot go further along the paths of

1 This equality within difference is contrary to what is said by Elisabeth Badinter, for whom complementarity of the sexes still brings inequality. *L'un est l'autre*, Ed. Odile Jacob, 1986.

modernity opened up by the author of the *Green Book*. In any case, the latter is without any doubt credited with authenticity by those women-symbols who are the women officers, the Rahibat, the members of the Revolutionary Committees, whom he has turned into both the vectors and the agents of his ideology.

These Libyan women, who more than any others share the faith of the inspiring Guide and are subject to his charisma, have contributed not a little to making the revolution sacred and to progress in the development of mentalities. Whether it was a question of shaping – one could say "cossetting" – the Libyan identity, of overcoming the generation conflict, of establishing religious belief by reinterpreting the message of Islam and the Arab culture across the tumults of the century, of conceiving in justice the participation in the production and management of the economy, but especially of imagining through the Jamahiryan concept the future of a stifled society – still stifled in its patriarchal straitjacket, and yet already in contact with liberties – the meeting between the revolutionary leader and the young generation of Libyan women provoked many more agreements than observers and analysts of modern Libya generally think.

Militants of the hard cores and the political networks, the new feminist élites have in many cases conciliated and reconciled, if not arbitrated in a sort of emotional logic the relationship between the "base" and the Leader, which they continue to energise in the main compartments of political life.

Ghadafi and Libyan women – those of his childhood and those of the Jamahirya, apparently united and inseparable – go forward together on the difficult paths of modernity. Are they, as they believe, opening up a new way not only for Libya but for the whole of humanity?

APPENDICES

Appendix A

TEST QUESTIONNAIRE
submitted to a sample of 183
civil and military students

  I. A girl wants to go to the Women's Military Academy, but her parents are totally opposed to this plan. She has not managed to persuade them. What should she do?

  1. She must give up the idea of enrolling.

  2. She must enrol nevertheless, hoping that her parents will change their minds later.

  II. A girl wants to put the money that she earns away (in the bank) so as to be able to buy a car, which she needs for her work. Her parents do not agree, they say that they have to share everything, that she must give her money to the family, and that she can just as well take the bus to get about. What should she do?

  1. She must give in to her parents and give up her savings account.

  2. She must put her money away nevertheless.

III A young woman officer is given an important job on a military base. She is married and has three children. One of the children falls ill, he needs his parents. Should she stay with him and cancel her work? Should she ask her husband to stay with the child? Or should she look for another solution?

1. She must cancel her work and stay with the child.
2. She must go to work and entrust the child to somebody.
3. The father must look after the child on this occasion.

IV. A young student officer wants to marry a military colleague, he understands her well and she is in love with him. Her parents are against this, as they want her to marry her cousin. She feels affection for her cousin with whom she gets on well, but she really loves her military colleague. What should she do?

1. She must obey her parents and marry her cousin.
2. She must follow her heart and marry the soldier.

V. A married woman, mother of three children, likes her work. She does not want to have any more children, as she thinks she would no longer have the time to work. Her husband, however, would like a large family, six or seven children, and he wants her to leave work, as he thinks it is more useful (for a woman) to have children than to work in an office. What should she do?

1. She must give up her work to have more children.
2. She must carry on working and tell her husband she is not having any more children.

VI. An officer couple, both captains, have four children. They work on a military base. War breaks out and they are each called to their respective units. What should they do?

1. Leave their children to other people.
2. Only the mother must stay with the children.
3. They must stay with their children in turn.

VII. A married woman, a mother, likes her work a lot. But, very tired by her double task at home and outside, she asks her husband, who is free every afternoon, to help her in her domestic chores. He refuses and says: "You only have to stay at home and leave work". What should she do?

1. She must give up work.
2. She must carry on working and neglect the housework a little.
3. She must put her children in a nursery.

VIII. The husband is in agreement that his wife, a doctor, exercises her profession. One day she has to go in a delegation with colleagues to a congress abroad for one week. Her husband does not want her to go, in fact he is jealous that she is going with other men that he does not know. What should she do?

1. She must go with the delegation all the same, if she has obtained an exit permit.
2. She must give up the idea of going to the congress.

IX. The husband earns a good salary, his wife, who works, also earns money. She intends to keep her salary for herself, as the household does not need it at all. The husband refuses, wanting them to share everything. What should she do?

1. She must give up her salary to her husband and the family.
2. She must give her husband at least part of her salary.
3. She must keep all her salary for herself.

X. A woman officer lives with her parents while carrying out her functions at the barracks. One day, she is posted to another town, far from her parents, and she is forced to take accommodation there. Her parents do not want her to live alone, they want her to resign from the army. What should she do?

1. She must terminate her contract with the army and resign.
2. She must accept her new posting and leave the family home, as her own career is at stake.

XI. In your opinion, is it normal that in a marriage with children, where both husband and wife work, the husband should help his wife:

To clean the house?	Yes/No
To do the washing?	Yes/No
To do the ironing?	Yes/No
To prepare the meals?	Yes/No
To look after the children?	Yes/No
To do the shopping?	Yes/No.

XII. By whom should the family budget be managed?

1. By the husband alone.
2. By the wife alone.
3. By the couple together.

XIII. Is it normal for the husband to go on holiday on his own, leaving his wife and children at home?
  1. Yes, that is normal and acceptable.
  2. Yes, but it must not happen too often.
  3. No, it is not acceptable.
XIV. In your opinion is a woman who goes out in public with her hair carefully covered to be thought more respectable than one who goes out with her hair free, even though correctly dressed?
  1. Yes, it is preferable for a woman to cover her head in public, she will be respected more.
  2. No, she can make herself be respected just as well without that, dress is not really important.

Appendix B

INTERVIEW WITH KHAIRIA, (1989) woman officer pilot

I. WMA diploma in 1982. Just completed training as a pilot.
Age: 26.
Origin: village close to the Tunisian border.
Composition of family: 6 children.
Father's profession: employed by Ministry of Health as a nurse.
Mother's profession: housewife, primary school level.
No soldiers in the family.

II. *Professional choice*
  – "My choice of a military career is an ideological choice
  – After the events in Lebanon, the Sabra and the Shatila camps, and when we learned of the 'defenceless' situation of the Palestinian and Arab women in general, I thought it was necessary for things to change; I wanted to take part in a movement to change the fate of Arab women and personally show that women can take part in everything, particularly in defending their homeland, themselves and their families. I wanted to become an example for other women.

241

– "No, my family weren't against it, my father even encouraged me. I liked the training at the WMA a lot. Then I worked for two years as a supervisor teaching in a secondary school. This school specialised in 'air defence'. In our country all the secondary schools have a speciality. The pupils are trained to be able to help and assist this or that weapon (ground assistance). It is our idea of the people at arms. The lessons are technical, we don't fly. But personally I really wanted to learn to fly. Then I was able to be trained as a "Mig" pilot, for 3 years, and I have just got my diploma. There are already several of us women pilots in Libya. There is also one woman pilot in the civil company, Libyan Arab Airlines.

– We get a diploma which is internationally recognised (on the basis of a certain number of hours flying time).

– Yes, after I joined the WMA, my mother also wanted to follow military training. She wanted to get closer to me.

– No, there is no contradiction between the army of the people and the regular army; we are the managers, the specialists for the army of the people".

IV. *Future plans*

– "I would like to get married one day, to a soldier, or a civilian, it doesn't matter, it all depends on the person. It's better to be married. But for the time being, I only think about my career. I want to carry on working in the army and make myself useful to my country. It is quite possible to combine work and housework; I know lots of women who manage to combine both. But you mustn't have too many children. Also, an understanding and co-operative husband.

– It is difficult to command men? No, not in the army; it's normal for a lower rank to obey a higher rank, man or woman. It's the same thing, the same military law".

V. *Personal opinions* (Women in the army)

– "It's an honour for women, how they have been allowed to join the army in Libya. It's also a duty for them as citizens to take part in the defence of their country. It's in fact a chance to expand the professional field for women; the army is a new professional area for women. It's therefore both an honour and a duty, and it's a sign that they can now work everywhere".

(A "liberated" woman)
— "Liberty is the most important thing in life for men and women. Liberty is the freedom to work, to choose one's own destiny, one's own way of life. The limits of this liberty are formed by religion and social norms. Traditions, the pressures exercised by the family still exist here, but they are reducing every day. Traditions must not be a brake on liberty. This said, it is in no way liberty as some European women imagine it. On the contrary, they become slaves to alcohol, tobacco, drugs, or discotheques. There is only one kind of liberty and only one definition of liberty; it is control of oneself".

Appendix C

LEGISLATION
relating to marriage and divorce

Law no. 10 of 19 Rajab 1393 (19 April 1984) relating to marriage and divorce contains 75 articles.

Objectives of the law

Its principal aim is to transform the inequality of rights between men and women which characterised the previous legislation. It therefore aims to establish an equivalence of rights, on a basis of reciprocity, between both sexes. As women have become complete citizens, the necessity for the double legislative status automatically disappears.

This law had been rejected several times by the General Popular Congress, with an overwhelming majority of male members, before being finally adopted in 1984 (it was applied retroactively for one year).

Terms of the law

The most notable terms of the law concern:

– the age of marriage for both partners; it is now fixed at 20; the court can, however, declare exceptions;

– the marriage contract; the woman was previously excluded from the contract negotiations (she was represented by her father or her guardian); now the contract is negotiated in her presence and with her personal participation, without limitation of title of the clauses likely to be agreed by one or the other of the partners (including, for example, the woman's right to exercise a profession, or the ban on the husband turning to polygamy);

– equality of rights; the law establishes reciprocity of obligations between the two partners.

However, the household expenditure remains the husband's responsibility (Qu'ranic obligation). The woman retains management of her personal property (a rule also in accordance with the Qu'ran).

The two partners are bound to abstain from causing mutual prejudice, material or moral. If this is not observed, divorce can be applied for, by the woman as well as the man.

If the husband is not in a position to provide for the maintenance of the household because of lack of resources (in the event of physical disability for example), the wife is supposed to have to participate financially in the expenses of the household.

She must also see to it that marital life runs harmoniously. She must take care of the children, of whom she will have custody in the event of divorce, whether this is applied for by her or her husband.

In the event of divorce, she automatically retains use of the family house, the furniture and the equipment, for her and the children. Custody of the children, regarded as a natural right, can only be withdrawn from her in the event of physical disability or moral unworthiness, according to the decision of the court, or again if she remarries, and then there are grounds for payment of alimony.

In the cases so defined, custody of the children will go, by order of preference, to the wife's mother; otherwise to the husband's mother.

So divorce, which must take place before a court, is not an absolute right of the husband (repudiation had been banned in Libya from the start of the Revolution), but a reciprocal right, for which the woman has the same power to apply as the man.

– As for the judicial procedures, the law of 1976 which excluded women from the magistrature was amended in 1988; women now have the same access to the magistrature as men (having being previously granted the right to exercise the profession of lawyer).

To sum up, we note that the new Libyan legislation (1984–1988) firstly introduces equality of rights and reciprocity between the partners, and secondly gives the woman (or her mother) a greater responsibility in the event of divorce. It remains to be said that Libyan legislation, based on the Sharia, can in no case contradict it. That is why the Qu'ranic rule about two witnesses for the woman (compared with only one for the man) and the Qu'ranic rule about reducing the share of the inheritance given to the woman to a half remain applicable.

As for corporal punishment (mutilations, stoning), it seems that they have no longer been applied since 1972. By the strictest respect for the conditions required (the thief's confession, or proof to establish that he did not need to steal), application of the Sharia tends to become practically impossible, the courts having been led more and more to judge according to the terms of a penal code largely inspired by Italian law.

So the law of 1984, which is in strict observance of the Qu'ranic rules, has complemented them – unless it has adapted them – to take account of the constraints and norms imposed by modern life.

Appendix D

THE GREAT GREEN CHARTER OF THE RIGHTS OF MAN OF THE JAMAHIRYAN ERA

The Libyan Arab people, meeting at the Basic Popular Congress,

Inspired by the first Declaration of the great revolution of Al Fateh (1 September 1969), which was the definitive triumph of liberty on this earth,

Directed by the principles of the historical Declaration of the establishment of the power of the people of 2 March 1977, an event which opened a new era crowning the uninterrupted struggle of humanity, throughout the centuries, and confirming its unceasing aspiration to liberty and emancipation,

Led by the *Green Book*, guide of humanity for the total deliverance from any power of individuals, of classes, of clans, of tribes or parties, and the path towards establishment of a society for all, where all human beings would be free and equal in the exercise of power and in the possession of wealth and arms,

In response to the constant encouragement of the internationalist leader, Moammar Qaddafi, founder of the Jamahiryan era who by his thought and his labour makes concrete the aspirations of the oppressed and the enslaved in the world, and who opens before peoples the path of change

249

by popular revolution, an essential instrument to establish the Jamahiryan society,

Convinced that the Rights of Man, suppliant of God on earth, cannot be the gift of a person nor exist in societies where exploitation and tyranny are practised, and can only be achieved by the victory of the popular masses over the oppressors and the disappearance of regimes which destroy liberty, that the establishment of the power of the popular masses will consolidate their existence on earth, when the sovereignty of the people will be exercised through the Popular Congresses, that human rights cannot be guaranteed in a world where there exist governors and governed, masters and slaves, rich and poor,

Aware that human misery can disappear, and the rights of man be affirmed, only by the edification of a Jamahiryan world where the people hold the power, the wealth and the arms; a world where governments and armies will disappear, and where communities, peoples and nations will get rid of any danger of war, a world of peace, respect, agreement and co-operation.

On the basis of the above and the decisions of the national and international Popular Congresses, held in the country and outside, the Libyan Arab people, guided by the famous slogan of Omar Ibn Al Khattab:

"Since when can we enslave men when their mothers brought them into the world free?"

words which were the first declaration of liberty and the Rights of man in the history of humanity,

Decide to promulgate the *Great Green Charter of Human Rights of the Jamahiryan Era*, the principles of which are as follows:

1. Democracy is the power of the people and not the expression of the people. The members of the Jamahiryan society declare that power belongs to the people. They exercise it directly, without intermediary or representatives in the popular congresses and the popular committees.

2. The members of the Jamahiryan society consider the life of the individual sacred and protect it. They forbid its alienation. Imprisonment can only be exercised against those for

whom liberty constitutes a danger or a contamination of others. The aim of punishment is to renew society, to protect its human values and its interests.

The Jamahiryan society proscribes punishments which attack the dignity and the integrity of the human being, such as forced labour or long-term imprisonment.

The Jamahiryan society proscribes all attacks, physical or mental, on the person of the prisoner. It condemns all speculations and experiments of any kind of which he could be the subject.

The punishment is personal and suffered by the individual following a criminal act on which it must depend.

The punishment and its consequences cannot extend to the family nor the persons close to the criminal. *"One only commits evil to one's own detriment and nobody will assume what he has not committed"*.

3. The members of the Jamahiryan society are, in times of peace, free in all their movements and in the choice of their residence.

4. Citizenship in the Jamahiryan society is a sacred right. Nobody can be deprived of it or have it removed.

5. The members of the Jamahiryan society forbid clandestine action and recourse to force in all its forms, violence, terrorism and sabotage.

These acts constitute a betrayal of the values and principles of the Jamahiryan society, which affirms the sovereignty of the individual in the Basic Popular Congresses, guaranteeing him the right to express his opinion publicly.

They reject and condemn violence as a means of imposing ideas and opinions.

They adopt democratic dialogue as the only method of debate and consider any hostile relation towards the Jamahiryan society linked to a foreign instance, whatever its form, as high treason against it.

6. The members of the Jamahiryan society are free to form unions, trade unions and leagues to defend their professional interests.

7. The members of the Jamahiryan society are free in their private acts and their personal relations.

Nobody can involve themselves therein, except at a complaint from one of the partners concerned or if the act and the relation attack or are prejudicial to society, or if they are contrary to its values.

8. The members of the Jamahiryan society consider the life of the human being to be sacred and protect it.

The objective of the Jamahiryan society is to abolish capital punishment.

To this end, the death penalty can only be exercised against an individual whose existence constitutes a danger or is deleterious to society.

The person condemned to death may request that his sentence be lightened or, instead of his life, offer a personal tribute.

The court may commute the penalty if this decision is not prejudicial to society or if it is not contrary to human values.

The members of the Jamahiryan society condemn the application of the execution of capital punishment by repugnant methods, such as the electric chair, the use of toxic gas or injections.

9. The Jamahiryan society guarantees the right to plead and the independence of the judicial system.

Each of its members is entitled to a fair and complete trial.

10. The judgements of the members of the Jamahiryan society are based on sacred law, religion or custom, the terms of which are stable, unchangeable and for which there can be no substitute.

They declare that religion is an absolute belief in the divinity and a sacred spiritual value. It is personal to each person and common to everyone. It is a direct relationship with the Creator, without intermediary.

The Jamahiryan society proscribes its monopoly and its exploitation for purposes of subversion, fanaticism, sectarianism, partisan in spirit and fratricidal war.

11. The Jamahiryan society guarantees the right to work. It is a right and a duty for everyone, in the limits of one's personal effort or in association with others. Everybody has the right to exercise the work of their choice.

The Jamahiryan society is one of partners and not one of paid employees. Ownership, the fruit of labour, is sacred and protected, it can only be attacked in the public interest and with fair compensation. The Jamahiryan society is free from the slavery of salaries, stating the right of everybody over their labour and protection. Only those who produce consume.

12. The members of the Jamahiryan society are liberated from any feudalism. The land is nobody's property. Each person has the right to exploit it and to benefit from it by labour, agriculture or animal-keeping, throughout his life, that of his heirs, and within the limits of his effort and the satisfaction of his needs.

13. The members of the Jamahiryan society are free from any rent. A house belongs to the person who lives in it. It enjoys a sacred immunity in respect of rights of neighbourhood: "Your close neighbours or distant neighbours". The residence cannot be used to harm society.

14. The Jamahiryan society is united. It guarantees everyone a worthy and prosperous life and a developed state of health, so as to achieve a society of healthy people. It guarantees protection of childhood, motherhood, old age and of invalids. The Jamahiryan society is the guardian of all those who do not have a guardian.

15. Education and knowledge are natural rights for everyone. Any individual has the right to choose his education and the knowledge which suits him, without imposed constraint or orientation.

16. The Jamahiryan society is the society of goodness and of noble values. It considers ideals and human principles sacred. Its aim is a humanitarian society where aggression, war, exploitation and terrorism will be banished and where there will be no difference between great and small.

All nations, all peoples, and all national communities have the right to live free, according to their options and the principles of self-determination. They have the right to establish their national entity. Minorities have the right to safeguard their entity and their heritage. The legitimate aspirations of the latter cannot be repressed. Neither can they be assimilated by force into one or several different nations or national communities.

17. The members of the Jamahiryan society affirm the right of each person to profit from the benefits, the advantages, the values and the principles which are obtained for him by agreement, cohesion, union, affinity and the affection of the family, the tribe, the nation and humanity.

To this end, they work to establish the natural national entity of their nation and support all those who fight to achieve this aim.

The members of the Jamahiryan society reject any segregation between men due to their colour, their race, their religion or their culture.

18. The members of the Jamahiryan society protect liberty. They defend it everywhere in the world.

They support the oppressed, and encourage all peoples to confront injustice, oppression, exploitation and colonialism. They encourage them to combat imperialism, racism and fascism, in accordance with the principle of the collective struggle of peoples against the enemies of liberty.

19. The Jamahiryan society is a society of splendour and fulfilment. It guarantees each person the right of thought, creation and innovation. The Jamahiryan society works for the development of the sciences, the arts and literature. It guarantees they will be disseminated among the popular masses so as to prohibit any monopoly on them.

20. The members of the Jamahiryan society affirm the sacred right for men to be born into a coherent family, where motherhood, fatherhood and brotherhood are given to him. Fulfilment of the human being is only in compliance with his nature if it is assured by natural motherhood and feeding. The child must be brought up by its mother.

21. The members of the Jamahiryan society, men or women, are equal in everything which is human. The distinction of rights between men and women is a flagrant injustice which nothing justifies.

They proclaim that marriage is a fair association between two equal partners.

Nobody can conclude a marriage contract by constraint, nor divorce in any other way than by mutual consent or by a fair judgement.

It is unfair to dispossess the children of their mother, and the mother of her home.

22. The members of the Jamahiryan society considers servants as the slaves of modern times, enslaved by their masters.

No law governs their situation, and they have no guarantee

nor protection. They live under the arbitrary nature of their masters, and are victims of tyranny. They are forced, by necessity and in order to survive, to carry out work which ridicules their dignity and human feelings.

For this reason, the Jamahiryan society proscribes recourse to servants in the home. The house must be maintained by its owners.

23. The members of the Jamahiryan society are convinced that peace between nations can guarantee them prosperity, abundance and harmony.

They call for an end to the trade of arms and their manufacture for purposes of exploitation. The arms industry constitutes a waste of wealth of societies, a burden on individual taxpayers, causing the spread of destruction and annihilation in the world.

24. The members of the Jamahiryan society call for the suppression of nuclear, bacteriological and chemical weapons and any other means of massive extermination and destruction.

They call for elimination of all the existing stocks, for the preservation of humanity from the dangers represented by the waste from nuclear power stations.

25. The members of the Jamahiryan society undertake to protect their society and political system based on popular power.

They also undertake to safeguard its values, principles and interests. They regard collective defence as the only means to preserve them.

They think that the defence of the Jamahiryan society is the responsibility of every citizen, man or woman. Nobody can have a substitute when confronted with death.

26. The members of the Jamahiryan society commit themselves to the bases of this charter.

They do not allow them to be infringed and forbid themselves any act contrary to the principles and rights that it guarantees.

Each person has the right to plead under the law for the purpose of reparation of any attacks on the rights and liberties that it announces.

27. The members of the Jamahiryan society offer the world, and with pride, the *Green Book*, the guide and path of

emancipation for the acquisition of liberty. They announce to the popular masses the advent of a new age, when corrupt regimes will be abolished and from which any trace of tyranny and exploitation will be extirpated.

The General Congress of the People of the
Popular and Socialist Libyan Arab Jamahirya.
Baida, 28 Ghawal 1397 from the death of the Prophet
12 Assayf/June 1988

Bibliography

A. WORKS AND ARTICLES QUOTED IN THE TEXT

- D. Abrous: *L'honneur face au travail des femmes en Algérie*, Thèse de 3e cycle, 1985.
- S.E. Asch: *Effects of group pressure on the modification and distortion of judgment*, 1951.
- E. Badinter: *L'un est l'autre*, Ed. O. Jacob, 1986.
- H. Barrada, M. Kravetz et M. Whitaker: *Kadhafi – Je suis un opposant à l'échelon mondial.* Coll. "les grands entretiens", Ed. P.M. Favre, Lausanne, 1984.
- R. Bastide: *Le sacré sauvage*, Payot, 1975.
- J. Bearman: *Quadafi's Libya*, Zed books, London, 1986.
- J. Berque: *Les arabes d'hier à demain*, Ed. du Seuil, Paris, 1962.
- T. Ben Jelloun: "Contre la misère politique", *Le Monde*, juillet 1989.
- J. Bessis: *La Libye contemporaine*, Ed. l'Harmattan, 1986.
- M. van Bockstaele et P. Schein: "Limites des négociations et négociations des limites", *Sociologie du travail* n° 11, Ed. du Seuil, 1977.
- F. Braudel (sous la direction de): *La Méditerranée*, Ed. Arts et métiers graphiques, 1988.
- J.P. Charnay: *L'Islam et la guerre*, Ed. Fayard, Paris, 1986.
- R. Charvin et J. Vignet-Zurz: *Le syndrome Kadhafi*, Ed. Albatros, Paris, 1987.
- P.H. Chombart de Lauwe, et Collab.: *Images de la femme dans la société*, Ed. Ouvrières, 1964.
- M. Djaziri: *Le système politique libyen*, Thèse de Doctorat Université de Lausanne, 1987.
- L. Festinger: *A theory of cognitive dissonance*, Eveston, Ill. Row, Peterson, 1953.

- M. Hussein: *Versant sud de la liberté, essai sur l'émergence de l'individu dans le tiers-monde*, Ed. La découverte, 1989.
- Cl. Julien: "Respect", *Le Monde diplomatique*, juin 1989.
- Mu'ammar El Kadhafi: *Es-sijill al-qawmi*, Tripoli, 1970–1989.
- Mu'ammar El Kadhafi: *Le Livre Vert*, t. 1 (la démocratie), t. 2 (questions économiques), t. 3 (questions sociales). Ed. Cujas.
- H. Mattes: *Von der Prätorianer Garde König Idris I zum Konzept des Bewaffneten Volkes*, Orient Deutches Orient-Institut, Hamburg, 1985.
- F. Mernissi: *Le harem politique – Le Prophète et les femmes*, Albin Michel, Paris, 1987.
- E. Reynaud: *Les femmes et l'armée: l'exemple américain de l'intégration des femmes dans l'armée*, Institut Français de Polémologie, 1984.
- L. Saada: *La geste hilalienne – version de Bou Thadi*, Gallimard, 1985.
- A. Roussillon: compte rendu du colloque tenu au Caire en 1984 sur les nouveaux fondamentalistes: "*Authenticité et Modernité: les défis de l'identité dans le monde arabe*". Monde Arabe Maghreb-Machrek, n° 107, Troisième trim. 1985.
- F. Soudan: *Kadhafi, vingt ans de solitude*, Jeune Afrique, juin 1989.
- Ch. Souriau: *Femmes en politique autour de la Méditerranée*, ouvrage collectif, L'Harmattan, Paris, 1980.
- Z. Zohri et S. Azzi: *Le rôle économique et social dans la dynamique sociale*, Tripoli, 1983.

B. *WORKS ON LIBYA*

1. *Publications du Centre Mondial d'Etudes et de Recherches sur le Livre Vert:*

- *Commentaires sur le Livre Vert* (2 volumes), Tripoli 1984 et 1987.
- *La culture et le pouvoir: égalité*, Tripoli 1985.
- Davis: *Principle and practice of government in Qadhafi's Libya: Education*, Tripoli, 1984.
- *La Grande Charte Verte des Droits de l'Homme de l'ère jamahiryenne*, Tripoli, 1988.
- *Pensée Jamahiryenne*, n° 1, Janvier-Mars 1984 (Ire année).
- *Qadhafi's ideology: Theory and practice*, 1984.
- Actes des colloques sur le *Livre Vert*: (Benghazi 1979, Madrid 1982, Belgrade 1982, Benghazi 1983, Paris 1984).

2. *Other publications*

- Alawda: *Thus spoke Colonel Muammar Kadhafi*, Beirut Lebanon, 1974.
- Mohammad Annane: *Libya of Idris el Senoussi*, Beirut, Systeco, 1968.
- P. Audibert: *Libya*, Paris 1978, Ed. Seuil, Collection "Petite Planète".
- A.M. Ashinrakis: *La lutte pour la liberté de la Jamahirya libyenne*, Malta, 1978.
- M. Bianco: *Kadhafi, messager du désert*, Ed. Stock, 1974.
- H. Bleuchot: *Chroniques et documents libyens 1969–1980*, Ed. du CNRS, Paris, 1983.

- A. Cacchia: *Libya under the second Ottoman occupation (1835–1911)*, Tripoli, Government Press, 1945.
- A.M. Cazalis: *Kadhafi, le templier d'Allah*, Gallimard, 1974.
- Centre de recherches et d'études sur les sociétés mediterranéennes: *La Libye nouvelle, rupture et continuité*, Ed. du CNRS, 1975.
- J. Cooley: *Kadhafi: Vent de sable sur la Libye*, Ed. Robert Laffont, 1982.
- S. Dearden: *Nest of corsairs; the fighting Karamanlis of the Barbary Coast*, London, John Murray, 1976.
- M.K. Deeb and M.J. Deeb: *Libya since the revolution, aspects of social and political development*, Praeger special studies publishers, New York, 1982.
- L.C. Freud: *Annales tripolitaines*, Paris, 1927.
- R. First: *The elusive revolution*, Harmondsworth, 1974.
- Y. Gazzo: "Pétrole et développement: le cas libyen", Ed. Economica, 1979.
- H. Gueneron: *La Libye*, Collection "Que sais-je?", n° 1634, PUF, 1978.
- Dr. H. Habib: *Libya. past and present*, Adam Publishing House, Malta, 1982.
- M. de Mathuisieux: *A travers la Tripolitaine, Paris, 1903.*
- M. Kikhia: *Le nomadisme pastoral en Cyrénaique septentrionale*, Aix-en-Provence, 1968.
- R. Micacchi: *La Tripolitania, sotto il dominio dei Caramanli*, Roma, 1936.
- F. Muscat: *My president, my son . . . or one day that changed the history of Libya*, Adam Publishers, Malta, 1974.
- *Omar Mukhtar e la riconquista fascista della Libia*, Ouvrage collectif, Ed. Marzorati, 1981.
- A.M. Scott: *Procès á Khedafi*, Paris, S.E.F. Philippe Daudy, 1973.
- C. Souriau: *Libye: l'économie des femmes*, Ed. de L'Harmattan, 1984.
- F. Tondeur: *Libye, royaume des sables*, Ed. Fernand Nathan, 1969.
- M. el Wafi: *Charles Feraud et la Libye*, Malta, 1977.
- H. Willard: *Libya. The new Arab Kingdom of North Africa*, Cornell University Press, Ithaca, 1956.
- J. Wright: *Libya*, London, 1969.

3. *Miscellaneous articles*

- R. Abou-El-Haj: "An agenda for research in history: the history of Libya between the sixteenth and nineteenth centuries", *Int. J. Middle East Stud.*, USA, 1983.
- "L'annuaire de l'Afrique du Nord". Edité par le CNRS (Nombreux articles sur la Libye de H. Bleuchot, T. Monastiri, C. Souriau, L. Talha . . .).
- M. Attir: "Ideology, value changes and women's social position in Libyan society", *Women and the family in the Middle East*, Ed. Fernea, USA, 1985.
- Hervé Bleuchot et Yolande Martin: "Libye", *La formation des élites maghrébines*, L.G.D.J., 1972.
- H. Bleuchot: "Les fondements de l'idéologie du Colonel Mouammar el Kadhafi", *Maghreb Machrek* (62), mars–avril 1974.
- H. Bleuchot et T. Monastiri: "Le régime politique libyen et l'Islam",

Pouvoirs, revue française d'études constitutionnelles et politiques, n° 12, 1983.
- J.-P. Charnay: "Le Kadhafisme", *Esprit*, 1981.
- O. Fathally and M. Palmer: "Opposition to change in rural Libya", *Int. J. Middle East Stud.* II, Vol. 11, n° 2, USA, 1980.
- O. Fathally, M. Palmer, R. Chackerian: "Political development and bureaucracy in Libya", 1977, Lexington Books.
- O. Fathally, M. Palmer: "Political development and social change in Libya", 1980, Lexington Books.
- M. Fikry: "La femme et les conflits de valeurs en Libye", *Revue de l'Occident Musulman et de la Méditerranée*, n° 18, 1974, pp. 93–110.
- M. Graeff-Wassink: "Femme et révolution en Libye", *Les cahiers de l'Orient*, n° 6, Paris, juin 1987.
- A.A. El-Hammali: "Aspects of modernization in Libyan communities. Social and Economic Development of Libya", Middle East and North African Studies Press Limited, USA, 1975.
- "Libye 1978–1981", n° spécial de *Maghreb Machrek*, 3° trim, 1981.
- "La Libye", *Le Monde* – dossiers et documents n° 81 – Mai 1981.
- Dossier de travail: "La Libye en 1976", Services d'information et de diffusion du Premier Ministre, mars 1976.
- Mead, Richard and George, Alan: "The women of Libya", *Middle East International*, n° 25, July 1973.
- A.E. MeyerL *Islamic law in Libya: analyses of selected laws enacted since the 1969 revolution*, School of Oriental and African Studies, Department of Law, 1977.
- Miladi, Khadija: "Interview on the Status of Women in Libya", *Women International Network News*,3, 2, 1977.
- J. Roumani: "From republic to Jamahirya; Libya's search for political community", *The Middle East Journal*, Vol. 37, USA, 1983.
- M.L. Samman: "Activité économique des femmes du tiers-monde et perspectives de baisse de leur fécondite", *Revue Tiers-Monde*, Tome XXIV, n° 94, 1983.
- C. Souriau: "La société féminine en Libye", *Revue de l'Occident musulman et de la Méditerranée* (6), 1969.
- C. Souriau: "Femmes libyennes et politique", *Revue française d'études politiques méditerranéennes*, 3° trimestre 1977.

C. POLITICAL, SOCIOLOGICAL AND PSYCHO-SOCIOLOGICAL STUDIES

1. *Various works*

- Dr. K. Abraham: *Psychoanalyse et culture* (textes réunis), Petite bibliographie Payot, Paris, 1966.
- S. Abou: *L'identité culturelle*, Ed. Anthropos, Paris, 1981.
- B. Badie: *Contestation en pays islamique* (2 vol.) Publication du CHEAM, Paris, 1984.
- E. Badinter: *Emilie, Emilie, l'ambition féminine au* XVIIIe *siècle*, Ed. Flammarion, Paris, 1983.

– E. Badinter: *L'un est l'autre*, Ed. Odile Jacob, 1986.
– T.B. Bottomore: *Elites et société*, Ed. Stock, Paris, 1964.
– F. Burgat: *L'Islamisme au Maghreb*, Ed. Karthala, Paris, 1989.
– P.-H. Chombart de Lauwe: *Pour une sociologie des aspirations*, Ed.
  Denoël-Gonthier, 1971.
– P.-H. Chombert de Lauwe: *La culture et le pouvoir*, Ed. Stock, 1975.
– Col. R. Caire: *La condition féminine dans les armées* (résume d'une thèse)
  A. A. n° 56, Décembre 1980.
– D. Chevallier (en collab.): *Renouvellements du monde arabe 1952–1982*,
  Ed. Armand Colin, Paris, 1987.
– L. Dispot: *Ma machine à terreur – révolution française et terrorismes*, Ed.
  Grasset et Fasquelle, 1978.
– J. Duvignaud: *Le don du rien*, Ed. Stock, Paris, 1977.
– B. Etienne: *L'islamisme radical*, Ed. Hachette, Paris, 1987.
– B. Etienne: *La France et l'Islam*, Ed. Hachette, 1989.
– "Femmes de la Méditerranée". Diff. Chiron, Peuples méditerranéens
  22–23, Paris, 1983.
– "La Formation des Elites politiques maghrébines". Centre de recherche
  et d'études sur les sociétés méditerranéennes, Aix-en-Provence. Ed.
  CNRS, Paris, 1973.
– L. Granger: *La communication dans le couple*, Les Editions de l'homme,
  Montréal, 1980.
– J.P. Klein: *Les masques de l'argent*, Ed. Laffont, Paris, 1984.
– I. Madkour: *"Islam et évolution"*, *Int. J. Middle East Stud.*, Vol. II, n° 4.
  USA, 1980.
– C. Magaud: *De la violence internationale*, Ed. Economica, Paris, 1988.
– M. Mead: *L'un et l'autre sexe, les rôles d'homme et de femme dans la société*,
  Ed. Denoël-Gonthier, 1975.
– A. Michel: *Activité professionelle de la femme et vie conjugale*, CNRS,
  1974.
– J. Minces: *La femme dans le monde arabe*, Ed. Mazarine, Paris, 1981.
– F. Mernissi: *Sexe, idéologie, islam*. Trad. Brower, Pelletier, Ed. Tierce,
  Paris, 1987.
– G. Montmollin: *L'influence social: facteurs et théories*, PUF, 1977.
– E. Naraghi: *L'Orient et la crise de l'Occident*, Ed. Entente, Paris, 1977.
– C. Olivier: *Les enfants de Jocaste*, Ed. Denoël-Gonthier, Paris, 1980.
– R. du Pasquier: *L'Islam entre tradition et révolution*, Ed. Tougui, Paris,
  1987.
– *Peuples méditerranéens:* "Les femmes et la modernité", n° 44–45, Paris,
  Juillet–Decembre 1988.
– *Peuples méditerranéens:* "L'identité déchirée", n° 24, Paris, Juillet–
  Septembre 1983.
– *Peuples méditerranéens:* "Fin du national?", n° 35–36, Paris, Averil–
  Septembre 1986.
– A. Poitrineau: *Les mythes révolutionnaires – l'utopie et la mort*, Ed. P.U.F.,
  Paris, 1987.
– A.-M. Rocheblave-Spenlé: *Les rôles masculins et féminins*, Ed. Universi-
  taires, 1970.
– G. Rocher: *Introduction à la sociologie générale*, t. 1 – L'Action sociale, t. 2

- L'Organisation sociale, t. 3 - Le Changement social H.M.H., coll. "Points", 1970–1972.
- N. el Saadaoui: *La face cachée d'Eve*, Ed. des Femmes, Paris, 1982.
- *Sou'al* (numéro spécial): "L'Islamisme aujourd'hui", Ed. L'Association pour le développement de la culture et de la science dans le tiers-monde, Avril 1985.
- A. Taheri: *La terreur sacrée*, Ed. Sylvie Messinger (version français), 1987.
- *Women and the family in the Middle East*, Ouvrage collectif, Ed. E. Warnock Fernea University of Texas Press, USA, 1985.
- *Women in the Arab world*, Ouvrage collectif, Unesco, Paris, 1984.

2. *Revue articles*

- Bulletin d'Information des Etudes Féminines, Centre d'études féminines de l'Université de Provence.
- Comptes rendus des conférences sur *"L'accès de la femme aux responsabilités publiques dans le pays Méditerranées"*, FMVJ-Cités Unies.
- *Esprit* (divers articles).
- *Jeunes Afrique* (divers articles).
- *Maghreb, Machrek* (divers articles).
- *Peuples méditerranéens.*
- *Tiers-Monde* (divers articles).
- Unesco: Comptes rendus de divers séminaires internationaux ou nationaux concernant la femme.